What Would YOU Do if The Lights Went Out?

A Personal Guide to Emergency Preparedness

What Would YOU Do if The Lights Went Out?

A Personal Guide to Emergency Preparedness

By

Mark B. Szkolnicki

Canadian Cataloguing in Publication Data

Szkolnicki, Mark B.   1959 –
       What Would YOU Do If the Lights Went Out?
       A Personal Guide to Emergency Preparedness

ISBN 0-9782206-0-9

1. Emergency Management 2. Survival Skills I. Title
HV551.2.S98 2007

Acknowledgements
Book Design: Dennis Kashton
Emergency Photos: Gary M. Trask and Mark B. Szkolnicki
Publication Assistance by: Aivilo Press
Printed and Bound in Canada by Hignell Printers

Disclaimer
While the information presented in this book is believed to be accurate and factual, and representative of the most current state of knowledge for the subject presented, the author and the publisher assume no liability for any damages resulting from errors, omissions, misinterpretation, use or misuse of the information presented.

Published By

PALADIN
Environmental Publishing
155, 51551 Range Road 212A Sherwood Park, Alberta, Canada
Telephone: 780-922-0072 Toll Free: 1-877-464-5900

TABLE OF CONTENTS

FOREWARD 1

INTRODUCTION 13
   Make a list and pre-plan 18
   Stockpile resources 22
   Gather and prepare information 32

PREPAREDNESS IN THE HOME 39
   Physical supplies and equipment 39
   Food supplies 42
   Water supplies 45
   Water treatment 48
   Heating and fuel supplies 50
   First aid supplies 50
   Fire protection equipment 52
   Other emergency preparedness items ...55
   Emergency information 57
      First aid 57
      Phoning for help 58
      Contact points 60
      Emergency contact card 62
      Insurance 64
      Personal emergency plan 66
      Evacuation checklist 70
      Important documents......................71
      Utilities.. 73
   Emergency pre-planning when building a home ...74
   Maintenance or modification 77
      General maintenance for emergencies 77
      Maintenance for fires in the home 78
      Maintenance for forest fires 79
      Preparing for earthquakes............................. 80
      Hurricanes or windstorms 81
      Maintenance for blizzards or ice storms............81
   In an actual emergency in the home 83
      If a medical emergency occurs 83

If a power disruption occurs 85
If a heating disruption occurs 89
If water supply is disrupted or contaminated 93
Water management 94
Keeping clean 95
Managing sewage 96
If a fire is occurring in the home 98
If a severe thunderstorm occurs 99
If a flood warning is issued 100
TORNADOS 104
If a tornado occurs 105
HURRICANES OR TYPHOONS 107
If a hurricane is predicted for your area 107
If a windstorm is forecast for your area 110
If an earthquake occurs in your area 111
If a forest fire occurs 114
If a blizzard or ice storm is forecast 116
If extremely hot weather is occurring 117
General heat preparedness measures 117
If a chemical or petroleum release occurs near your
home or near your community 121
Evacuation 124

PERSONAL PREPAREDNESS IN YOUR OFFICE 129
Supplies and equipment 130
Emergency information 132

TRAVEL PREPAREDNESS – ROAD VEHICLES 134
Supplies and equipment 134
Emergency information 137
Regular travel 138
Travel on long trips 139
In an actual emergency 143
If caught in severe weather 144
If a tornado is spotted while traveling 146
If flash flooding occurs while traveling 147
If an earthquake occurs while traveling 149
If your vehicle is stuck or has mechanical problems 150
If stranded in a remote area 151
If you are lost 153

TRAVEL PREPAREDNESS - BOATS **154**
Supplies and equipment **154**
Training and information **159**
Boating safety 159
Radio communication..................................... 161
First aid 161
For your trip **162**
Prior to regular travel via boat 162
Prior to travel on long trips via boat 163
While traveling to your destination via boat 167

PREPAREDNESS FOR OUTDOOR ACTIVITIES **168**
Supplies and equipment **168**
Survival skills and information 171
Communicate where you are 174
Monitor weather conditions 175
During your outdoor trip 175
When camping overnight 177

TRAVEL PREPAREDNESS – OTHER COUNTRIES ... **179**
Prior to traveling to other countries **179**
Emergency travel supplies and equipment **184**
Travel emergency kit 184
Medications 186
Information 188
During Your Trip **188**
While traveling in a foreign country 188
Limiting the possibility of a travel related
medical emergency occurring 190

PREPAREDNESS FOR SPECIAL NEEDS **191**
Personal assessment for special needs **192**
Personal emergency plan for special needs 194
Emergency information 194
Medical information 195
Evacuation plan 196
Support network for special needs 198
**Emergency preparedness for infants
and children** **202**
Supplies and equipment 203
Information 204

Child proofing to prevent emergencies 207
In an actual emergency affecting your family 209
Emergency preparedness for the elderly **212**
Supplies and equipment 213
Emergency preparedness for a
person with disabilities **214**
Supplies and equipment 214
Emergency preparedness for pets **219**
Supplies and equipment 221
Emergency information 223
Support network 225
If you must evacuate and bring a pet 228
If you must leave your pet behind 229
After an emergency where a pet is involved 231

PERSONAL PREPAREDNESS – PANDEMICS........... **232**
Pandemic Pre-Planning **234**
Supplies and equipment 235
If a pandemic does occur 237

NEW AGE EMERGENCY PREPAREDNESS **244**
Flashlights / spotlights **244**
Light sticks **245**
Radios **246**
Blankets **247**
Standalone alternative power sources **247**
Power inverters **248**
Portable power packs **249**
Personal communicators **250**
Battery back-ups **252**
Water purification devices **254**

ADDITIONAL REFERENCES **255**

To Anne

My partner in personal emergency preparedness
Who believed this book could also help others

FOREWARD

In the last few years in North America, there have been ice storms in Quebec, and the events at the World Trade Center in New York on September 11, 2001. Power outages occurred which affected 50 million people for days, in the northeastern United States and Canada. Major forest fires, have devastated many parts of Canada and the United States. Widespread boil water orders have been issued as a result of flash flooding due to exceptionally heavy rainfall in British Columbia.

The effects of Hurricane Juan in the Maritimes, Hurricane Charley in Southern Florida and the devastation of New Orleans and other communities by Hurricane Katrina have all reached national and international attention. Affects of hurricanes, blizzards, tornados, fires, floods, earthquakes, and other disasters have been felt around the world.

While municipalities, provinces, states and federal agencies are constantly planning and implementing actions to mitigate the affects of these emergencies, I have been struck by the fact that most individuals are totally unprepared for dealing with emergencies that affect them personally.

Government agencies can and do provide resources to aid and comfort the public. However, in a widespread emergency, with major implications, you may be required to function on your own, with your own resources, until help arrives. This may mean living without all the comforts we take for granted, like a constant supply of electricity, heat, or clean water.

Fuel for vehicles as well as food supplies may be affected. Modern conveniences like ATM machines or credit verification machines may be shut down and off line, preventing you from accessing any money from your accounts.

The affects of major emergencies may last for a few hours, or extend to several days or even weeks. Smaller emergencies, of short duration, could also occur, affecting you and those around you, requiring you to take immediate action to provide comfort and aid.

In this guide, I have attempted to compile useful, practical information, for a variety of situations, to help you understand the principles of emergency preparedness. The information presented is based on advice drawn from a variety of organizations, agencies and respected individuals in the emergency response field, as well as my own personal experience as an emergency responder and planner. Hopefully you will find this information useful if an emergency affects YOU.

Mark Szkolnicki, January 2008

INTRODUCTION

This handbook has been prepared to provide some helpful tips and advice on how you can prepare for and deal with an emergency which affects you personally

Throughout most of recorded history, individuals have relied on their own skills, ingenuity and resources to survive and prosper. In emergency situations, they continued to be self reliant, functioning with minimal aid from outside sources, living off the land as necessary.

In our modern day technological society we have become more and more reliant on others to provide for our daily needs. Others provide the bulk of our food, and our source of fuel for heating and for vehicles. Others provide electrical and communication services. Others even manage our financial resources.

When everything works smoothly and functions normally in society, we tend to take for granted that all these services exist. We forget that they can easily be cut off, if an emergency occurs locally, or if a major emergency happens which has widespread repercussions.

Grocery stores, shops, gas stations and financial institutions may be closed. Disruptions to gas, water, and electrical systems may occur temporarily, or for an extended period of time. Communications over a wide area may be cut off completely, and even short distance communications may be difficult.

Medical aid and resources may be overwhelmed in a major emergency, where widespread injuries have occurred.

Emergency agencies funded by municipal, provincial, state and federal governments do exist, and do plan for response to emergencies. However, these resources can be stretched to the limit in the initial stages of a localized emergency and may be strained for a significant period of time in a major emergency. Individuals, by necessity, may be forced to rely on their own resources on a temporary basis, until services can be restored.

This is why personal emergency preparedness is so important.

The amount of preparedness required for any individual, family, or group of individuals is dependent on various factors including:

- **The number of people** who may be affected by an emergency
- **The type of activities** you undertake on a regular basis
- **The types of emergencies** which can specifically affect you or your community, based on your locale

Every emergency described in this guide may not affect every individual. You should plan for emergencies that can reasonably occur, based on your personal circumstances.

This guide takes a practical approach to personal emergency preparedness. Preparedness for an emergency is not a complex task. However, it does require some commitment, time and effort, both initially and on an on-going basis, to maintain at least a basic level of emergency support for you and your family.

You may find that many of the elements suggested in this guide are already being undertaken, as part of your normal activities, and the items suggested are merely good common sense. However, I am reminded of a quote, which I read once, which describes this situation perfectly – "Common sense, how common is it?"

Common sense assumes that all individuals have the same level of knowledge and understanding related to a particular subject, and that all individuals can make an informed decision, based on the information they can obtain easily and quickly. However, if you don't even know the right questions to ask, it may be difficult to prepare for an emergency. Hence, the information presented in this guide.

Emergencies are unpredictable. Personal emergency resources cannot be made to appear magically, only when an emergency does occur. Basic levels of emergency preparedness can be achieved with a minimal amount of effort and financial commitment. As a minimum, every household should have a basic emergency kit stored in your home and in your vehicles.

In this guide I will also describe some options for more advanced preparation, if an individual or family wishes to undertake additional steps to enhance their ability to prepare for an emergency, or if your circumstances require it.

In an emergency situation, whether personal or widespread, it should be remembered that three priorities exist – protecting life, protecting property and protecting the environment. However, it must also be remembered that the ultimate priority is PROTECTING LIFE.

Personal emergency preparedness activities and advice provided in this guide focus on protecting your life as well as the lives of your family, by providing a temporary life support environment using your own personal resources. Think of it as "personal first aid", pending the arrival or setup of emergency support systems by local government officials, and the restoration of normal services.

REMEMBER – PREPARING FOR A PERSONAL EMERGENCY DEPENDS ON YOU!

Where to Start?

Personal emergency preparedness starts with
determining what emergencies could
occur, and how they would affect you
personally.

Two types of emergencies normally affect
an individual:

Emergencies which affect a person
indirectly, depriving them of essential
services.

These emergencies could include:

- **Fires or explosions** at an industrial facility, with widespread impact

- **Power failures** causing widespread blackouts

- **Major natural disasters** such as floods, forest fires, tornadoes, hurricanes, earthquakes, ice storms, and blizzards, which limit, damage or destroy essential services

- **Transportation accidents**, with release of toxic chemicals

Emergencies which affect a person *directly*, requiring an immediate response by the individual, to deal with the emergency.

These types of emergencies could include:

- **Medical emergencies** in the home

- **Fires in the home** or local area

- **Localized blackouts**

- **Vehicle accidents**, mechanical problems or being stranded in a vehicle in a remote location

- **Becoming lost** while camping or hiking

In all cases listed above, a person may have to rely on their own personal resources for a short time, or an extended period of time, prior to receiving external support from government or other agencies. The key to personal emergency preparedness is to determine what can go wrong, what you can do about it, and what items of preparedness you can undertake for that particular type of emergency.

Make a list and pre-plan

The best place to start preparing for an emergency is by sitting down for a few minutes, taking a pencil and paper and making some lists, to determine what you need to do to prepare for an emergency.

First, take a look inside and outside your home, and think about what could go wrong in the immediate area. Make a list of these emergencies.

Some of the more common emergencies that could affect you in the home include but are not limited to:

- **A fire in the home** or in a nearby building

- **An accident on a major road** near your home

- **A forest fire** near your home

- **A medical emergency** affecting one of your family or a neighbour

- **A flood caused by a heavy rainstorm** or snow melt in the spring, or from living close to a river or lake

- **A blizzard or ice storm** which prevents you from venturing outdoors

- **Localized blackouts** of short duration

- **A liquid chemical or petroleum release** from a gas station, plant or other facility (usually impacting homes in the immediate area surrounding the facility)

- **A release of a gaseous chemical or petroleum product** from a fire or accident at an industrial plant or facility, a gas station storing propane, or a train derailment or road accident involving dangerous goods

NOTE:

Gaseous releases may extend a significant distance from the release point, dependent on meteorological conditions at the time of release, thus extending the impact area.

Also, think about common emergencies that could affect you personally in other locations. These could include:

- **A breakdown in your vehicle** while away from home

- **A vehicle accident** which may affect you or another person while traveling

- **Being stranded** at the office in a major blizzard or other severe weather

- **An emergency at a summer cottage** or other vacation location

- **Travel** to other countries

- **Medical emergencies** affecting a neighbour or a family member living in another location away from you

If you undertake activities in remote locations, such as camping, hiking, skiing, trail biking, etc., you may also want to consider placing these activities on your list as well.

Next, think about major emergencies you've heard about, on the news in your area, or from other sources, and determine which of these emergencies may affect you. Think about what may happen to essential services and utilities. Also think about how you would communicate if standard electrical equipment, such as cordless telephones, plug-in radios and televisions are cut off.

Your location should also be considered, as part of your planning efforts. If you live in a city, extra supplies in an emergency may be more easily available, due to the concentration of manufacturers, warehouses and distribution centres in these areas. In populated areas in a major emergency, you will most likely receive timely support from local government agencies, in all but the most unusual circumstances.

In a remote location, these resources may not be readily available, requiring you to travel significant distances to obtain additional supplies. Help from government agencies may not be readily available. This should be taken into account in your planning efforts.

Consider any special needs or disabilities that you or your family may have. These needs could limit your ability to perform certain functions, or limit your ability to determine whether a hazardous condition has occurred. They may prevent you from evacuating an area where an emergency has occurred by yourself, or from taking care of yourself or others, without specialized supplies or equipment.

Every person and family is unique, for a variety of reasons. Therefore, ensure all special conditions and items that could be critical to your family's survival are taken into account.

As a final part of your pre-planning efforts, consider how many people may be affected by each of the emergencies you've listed, and for how long.

After you've made an assessment of the hazards that may affect you and listed your requirements, have a look at the various sections of this guide for more specific information, based on your own personal situation. Hopefully, you'll find some useful information and advice to supplement your current emergency preparedness efforts.

At a minimum, you should look at the "Supplies and Equipment" headings in various sections, for suggestions as to equipment or supplies you would want to have on hand if an emergency occurs. Make a "grocery list" of suggested items, as a reminder.

Plan your emergency preparedness efforts to suit your lifestyle. We are all involved with various activities in our busy lives, and there may be a lot of preparedness and planning activities that need to be done. Don't overwhelm yourself with details. Take it step-by-step and methodically, building up your resources steadily.

Consider your initial efforts as a project or a series of projects, and plan to undertake the required activities or gathering of resources over a month, two month or a six month period. Stretching out the time frame will also allow you to budget for purchasing additional needed resources, in a manner no different than any other home project.

Stockpile resources

 One of the most critical aspects of emergency preparedness is having the necessary resources available to you at all times, as an emergency can occur quickly, without warning. Stockpiling needed resources will go a long way towards enhancing your safety as well as your personal emergency preparedness.

Like any project around the home, stockpiling resources will take time and does require some effort. Some of the supplies and equipment identified on your "grocery list" may already be present in your home, vehicle or other locations you frequent. These items may only need to be gathered together in one place, for storage, in the event of an emergency. If selected items are not readily available, they may need to be purchased separately and acquired over time.

Consider stockpiling resources for your home first, as this is most likely where you spend most of your time away from work. Alternately, concentrate your emergency preparedness efforts around other activities and locations where you normally spend a lot of time.

Listed below is an example method of stockpiling resources for a basic emergency kit, and an initial emergency supply of food and water for one person in a home, to last three to four days. In the example, the supplies and equipment are gathered or purchased over a two-month (eight week) period.

Non-perishable food choices may be varied based on your own personal, cultural or dietary needs. Foods should be purchased that will suit you and your family's tastes and needs.

 **WEEK 1 – Grocery store**

Purchase the following for your emergency supplies:

- 1 jar of peanut butter
- 1 large can of juice
- 1 can tinned meat, fish or meat spread
- 1 box crackers
- **2-3 packages of drink or juice mixes,** tea bags, etc.
- **1 hand operated can opener** (if you do not have one to spare for the emergency kit)
- **1 permanent marker** (to keep with the emergency kit - for marking and dating containers)

Also do the following:

- **Determine where you want to store extra supplies of food and water.** Start storing your emergency food supplies in this location. Write the date you purchased the supplies, and rotate them regularly (rule of thumb – change designated non-perishable emergency food supplies at least every six to eight months)

- **Have a look in your home, and determine what type of clean containers you have available for storing extra water.** If none are available, consider saving some clean plastic containers, jugs or other suitable food grade containers from juice, milk or other consumable liquids, as they become empty

- **Store a gallon of clean water in your designated emergency kit location.** Mark the container as "Water" with your permanent marker, and date it, so you know when the water needs to be changed

- **Determine what emergency equipment you have, and what you may need to purchase.** As an example, older radios, flashlights, blankets or other items, which you don't use regularly, but which are still functioning properly, could be stored together in your emergency kit. If you determine you need to buy new items for your kit, you could budget these purchases over a few months

WEEK 2 – Hardware store

Purchase the following for your emergency kit:

- **Flashlight, and required batteries** (if you did not already find one for your emergency kit in the house)

- **A large waterproof box** of sufficient size to store your basic emergency kit items

- **Appropriate size waterproof boxes and bags** for organizing and storing small items in your kit

- **A "Swiss Army" style multiplex knife,** with appropriate tools, based on your needs (if you do not already have one to spare for your emergency kit)

- **Other required spare tools** (eg. a small tool kit containing screwdrivers, pliers and other general tools is a good idea, if these types of tools are not generally available in your home)

- **Matches** or a disposable lighter

Also do the following:

- **Start putting items you've designated as emergency supplies and equipment in the box you selected for your basic emergency kit.** Store the kit at a sufficient height above the ground to keep it dry in a flood, but also make it readily accessible to responsible members of your family in an emergency

- **Mark the items in your kit as "Emergency Kit or Emergency Use"** with your permanent marker, to ensure they are placed back in your emergency kit again, if used

WEEK 3 – Grocery store

Purchase the following for your emergency supplies:

- **1-2 cans of tinned fruit**

- **1 additional can of tinned meat**, fish or meat spread

- **1-2 cans of tinned soup**, preferably ready to eat (eg. no additional water required)

- **1 package dried pasta** or 2-3 packages of prepackaged pasta dinners

- **1 pack of toilet paper** (set aside 2-3 rolls for your emergency kit)

- **1-2 rolls of paper towels**

- **1 pack of candles** (to store in your emergency kit)

- **1 manual can opener** (if you do not have a spare)

- **1 manual bottle / can opener** (to open bottle tops and pierce cans)

Also do the following:

- **Put additional items you've designated as emergency supplies in your basic emergency kit box**

- **Store the extra food supplies** you've purchased for emergency use in the designated location

- **Store an additional gallon of clean water** in its designated location (mark the container with your permanent marker)

 **WEEK 4 – Specialty or hardware store**

Purchase the following for your emergency kit:

- **Portable radio and appropriate batteries** (if you did not already find one in the house)

- **A whistle or noise maker** for signaling (if you do not already have one)

- **Spare batteries of appropriate type** for all your emergency equipment

- **Blanket for emergency use** (if you do not already have one to spare for your kit)

- **3-4 garbage bags** and ties

Also do the following:

- **Put the equipment which you purchased or gathered above in your basic emergency kit box**

- **Mark the items purchased as "Emergency Kit or Emergency Use"** with your permanent marker, to ensure they are placed back in your emergency kit again, if used

 **WEEK 5 – Grocery store**

Purchase the following for your emergency supplies:

- ⊙ **1-2 cans of soup**, preferably "ready to eat"

- ⊙ **1 additional can of tinned meat**, fish or meat spread

- ⊙ **1-2 additional cans of tinned fruit**

- ⊙ **2-3 packaged instant meals**, "just add water" (eg. cup a noodles, instant pasta dishes)

- ⊙ **1 small bottle of plain bleach** (eg. with no colour safe additives, soap or other additives)

- ⊙ **1 eye dropper** (to use with bleach for water disinfection)

- ⊙ **1 pack of moist towelettes**

Also do the following:

- ⊙ **Put additional items you've designated as emergency supplies in your basic emergency kit box**

- ⊙ **Store the extra food supplies** you've purchased for emergency use in the designated location

- ⊙ **Store an additional gallon of clean water** in its designated location (mark the container with your permanent marker)

 **WEEK 6 – Drug store**

Purchase the following for your emergency supplies:

- **1 complete first aid kit**, sufficient for use by 1-2 persons, or the following supplies:
  - **Sturdy box** of sufficient size to store first aid supplies (preferably waterproof)
  - **Adhesive sterile bandages** of various sizes
  - **Triangular sterile cloth bandages**
  - **Fabric adhesive tape**
  - **Scissors**
  - **Tweezers**
  - **A supply of antiseptic towelettes**
  - **Soap**
  - **First aid manual** or handbook
  - **Fasteners** such as safety pins
  - **Pain relieving medications** such as Aspirin, Tylenol, Advil, etc.

- **Additional emergency medical supplies**, as appropriate for your needs, which may include but not be limited to:
  - **Antibiotic ointment**
  - **Tube of petroleum jelly** or other lubricant
  - **Thermometer**
  - **Medicine dropper** (eye dropper)
  - **Rubbing alcohol**

- Antacid tablets
- Anti-diarrhea medication
- Laxative medication
- **Feminine supplies** (as required)

Also do the following:

◎ **Determine where you want to place your first aid kit in the home.** The location should be easily accessible and at a proper height to allow responsible family members to access it in an emergency. Larger emergency kits sold in retail stores can usually be mounted on a wall for easy access

◎ **Store all your emergency medical supplies in the same location** for easy access, if possible

 WEEK 7 – Grocery store

Purchase the following for your emergency supplies:

◎ 1 pack plastic eating utensils

◎ 1 pack paper plates and plastic cups

◎ 1 box quick energy foods (eg. granola bars)

◎ Small supply of "comfort foods" (eg. cookies, candy bars)

Also do the following:

◎ **Put additional items you've designated as emergency supplies in your basic emergency kit box**

- **Store the extra food supplies** you've purchased for emergency use in the designated location

- **Store an additional gallon of clean water** in its designated location (date the container with your permanent marker)

- **Store a small amount of paper money and change** in your basic emergency kit (eg. small bag or roll of quarters)

WEEK 8 – Hardware store

Purchase the following for your emergency equipment:

- **Type ABC fire extinguisher(s)** (Underwriters Laboratory (UL) approved)

- **Large plastic bucket or pail,** with a sealable lid (for makeshift toilet facilities)

Also do the following:

- **Determine where you want to place your fire extinguisher in the home**

- **Mount the fire extinguisher on the wall using mounting hardware provided.** The location should be easily accessible and at a proper height to allow responsible family members, trained in its use, to access it in an emergency

- **Familiarize yourself with the instructions regarding the fire extinguisher's use** in an emergency. Show other responsible family members how to operate the extinguisher as required

Stockpiling resources in a manner similar to that described above should put you well on the way to preparing personally for an emergency in the home. Additional resources may need to be stockpiled and included if your situation includes individuals with disabilities, infants, the elderly, pets or other special needs.

Once you have prepared for an emergency in your home, start additional projects to create emergency kits and stockpile necessary resources for vehicles (eg. boats, cars) or for other activities you undertake on a regular basis (eg. camping, hiking, skiing, etc.) as required.

Specific information on recommended resources for a variety of situations, is provided in other sections of this book, and may be referred to for additional resource listings and suggestions.

Gather and Prepare Information

 Based on your initial emergency lists, prepared previously, you may also want to gather reference information to support your emergency preparedness efforts. As with stockpiling resources, gathering and preparing information can take some time and effort, so plan to undertake these activities over a reasonable period of time, based on your lifestyle and the requirements involved.

Make this into a project as well, which may be undertaken while you are stockpiling resources, or as a separate project, as required. The most time consuming activity will be related to gathering and preparing information for use in your home.

An example "To Do" list is presented below, for preparing and gathering information for your home over a two-month (eight week) period.

WEEK 1

To do:

◉ **Determine the appropriate emergency contact numbers** for your community. Consider including emergency numbers for utilities or other special circumstances as required

◉ **Determine an alternate emergency contact** (relative or friend) outside of the area where you live, who can be used as a check-in point for your family if you become separated and local communication is unavailable

◉ **Prepare a summary listing of all your emergency numbers**, and post them in visible places by the phones you use most frequently in your home. As a suggestion, include your address on the summary listing, as well as a brief description of how to get to the location, if finding the location is tricky. (See Figure 1 in this guide for a suggested format)

◉ **Go for a walk with your family**, or go out yourself, **and find the location of the nearest pay phone**, should you require one in an emergency

WEEK 2

To do:

- **Prepare a floor plan for your home,** outlining exit routes and indicate locations of your emergency kit, first aid kit and fire extinguishers

- **Make the floor plan a part of a one page emergency plan for the home.** Include on the plan a location and alternate location that you will go to, if you and your family must leave the house quickly, and become separated. Also include the telephone number of a local contact (friend or relative) that you will all phone if you can't reach the meeting point

- **Post a copy of your emergency plan in an easily accessible part of your home** and give a copy to all family members. Ensure that they all understand the information that is included in the emergency plan

WEEK 3

To do:

- **Gather and make a written inventory** of important documents in your home

- **Consider renting a safety deposit box** in a financial institution, or storing these documents in another secure off-site location

- **Photocopy these documents** and store the photocopies and a copy of the inventory in a sealed bag in your basic emergency kit

WEEK 4

To do:

- **Find out what emergency plans your children's school or day care have,** if operations in these institutions are disrupted. Find out where your children will be sent, if these institutions are required to close due to an emergency

- **Prepare a personalized emergency contact card for each of your children,** listing their name, address, home phone number, as well as emergency contact numbers at your workplace(s). Also list alternate emergency contact numbers (friends or relatives local and out-of-town) that can be notified in a major emergency, if you are missing or unavailable

- **Place a copy of the contact card in items that your children wear** or carry on a regular basis (eg. knapsacks, jackets, etc.)

WEEK 5

To do:

- **Determine what items you may need to take with you** if an emergency requires you to evacuate your home, and prepare an evacuation checklist

- **Consider photographing and creating an inventory of valuable jewelry or other precious items,**

35

and storing this information in a secure location (eg. safety deposit box), for insurance purposes

WEEK 6

To do:

- ⊚ **Gather information related to your family's medical requirements** including:
  - **Blood type**
  - **Medications taken on a regular basis**, including dosage, and frequency (eg. pills per day, week, etc.)
  - **Allergies to medications**, if known
  - **Contact number(s) for physicians**, optometrists, etc.
  - **Any special needs** for individual family members
  - **Any chronic medical conditions** that family members have (eg. asthma, heart condition, etc.)

- ⊚ **Prepare a small summary card**, listing the information above, and place it in your first aid kit

- ⊚ **Prepare a binder or folder of your pet's vaccination records**, and ID information (license I.D. tags, tattoo I.D. number (if applicable), and whether the pet has an ID chip implanted, if applicable

- ⊚ **Inquire about medical training organizations in your area** and consider signing up for First Aid and CPR training

WEEK 7

To do:

- Check insurance coverage for all emergencies which you determined could occur, and consider whether any exclusions to coverage exist, based on the location where you live

- Assess the need for additional insurance coverage and purchase, as appropriate

- Use a video recorder, or camera, to document the contents of your home for insurance purposes. Store the tape, or photos, in a safe location, where they cannot be damaged during an emergency. Consider making additional copies, and sending them to a friend or family member, for storage away from your home

WEEK 8

To do:

- Prepare an inventory list of items that should be present in your emergency kit. Tape this list to the box or place it inside the kit

- Prepare an inventory list of medical and first aid supplies which should be present in your first aid kit, and tape it inside or place it outside the kit

- Consider preparing a general inventory listing of emergency food and water supplies which should be present in your home (eg. 2 cans tinned meat, 3 cans tinned soup, 4 gallon jugs water etc.) and place it in or near the place where these emergency supplies are stored

Specific information for a variety of situations, including home preparedness, is provided in other sections of this book, and may be referred to for suggestions when preparing your own personal plan and for gathering emergency related information.

PREPAREDNESS IN THE HOME

We rely on our homes for many things. They are places for relaxation and sanctuary from a busy world. They are places of entertainment. They are also a basic life support system for us and our families, providing shelter, warmth, electricity, a source of water, sanitation and a place to store food and supplies.

In an emergency, which affects the area in which we live, damage, destruction or a power outage may deprive us of essential services for a short period or an extended period of time. It is therefore important to undertake some emergency preparedness activities, as it relates to our home.

Physical supplies and equipment

 A **basic emergency kit** should be stored in your home at all times, preferably in a location accessible to all members of your family, even when an emergency is not occurring.

Typical items stored in this type of basic kit include:

- **A battery powered flashlight**, or a flashlight with an alternate power source that does not require batteries

- **A battery powered portable radio**, or a radio with an alternate power source that does not require batteries

- **Fresh batteries** of appropriate type for each battery powered item

- **Warm blankets** (or "space blanket" type Mylar based substitutes)

- **A supply of moist towelettes** and/or facial tissues

- **Paper towels**

- **Toilet paper**

- **Candles**

- **A hand operated can opener**, to remove lids and make holes in cans containing liquids

- **Paper cups, plates and plastic utensils**

- **A multiplex pocketknife** (eg. "Swiss Army" type knife) or multi-tool which performs similar functions

- **A supply of matches** or a lighter, preferably in a waterproof case

- **A whistle** or other type of noisemaker

More advanced items which may be stored in kits of this nature include:

- **Water purification tablets** and/or a supply of basic household bleach (5.25% Sodium Hypochlorite), which **does not** contain any additives such as scent, "colour safe" additives or added cleaners

- **Clean glass or plastic eye dropper** (for adding bleach to water)

- **Small supply of high energy non-perishable foods** (in addition to non-perishable foods listed below)

- **Chemical light sticks** (for emergency lighting)

- **Heavy leather work gloves** (for clearing debris)

- **Safety goggles**

- **Antibacterial hand soap** (solid or liquid)

- **Writing supplies** (paper, pens, pencils)

- **Rope** (suitable length according to your needs)

- **Plastic sheeting**

- **Duct tape**

- **An emergency reference manual**

- **Plastic heavy duty garbage bags** and ties

- **A pail** with a tight fitting lid (for sanitation if toilet facilities are unavailable)

- **A small supply of paper money** and change (eg. roll of quarters and dimes for phoning)

- **Feminine supplies** (if required)

- **Spare tools** required for shutting utility valves or other tools you think you may require

- **Spare pair(s) of prescription glasses** for family members who require them, if you have older pairs available

- **Photocopies of important documents**, such as insurance policies

- **Barbeques or camp stoves**, and appropriate fuel

- **Power converters or inverters**, which allow small electrical devices to be charged or run from a vehicle battery

These more advanced items may already be in your home for normal use, and new items may not have to be purchased. However, consider storing spare items in one place, with your emergency kit, in the event that items used normally are inaccessible.

Try to keep at least a three-day supply of disposable items, which may be used, and preferably seven days or more if possible. Items stored in your emergency kit do not have to be new, or purchased specifically for that purpose. As example, older blankets or items of equipment, such as older portable radios, which are not used frequently, but which still function efficiently may be stored in the kit. Older prescription glasses, which have been replaced with newer glasses, could also be stored in your emergency kit.

Try to keep all the items, which form part of your emergency kit, in the same location, preferably in a sturdy bag or box, to ensure they are available in the case of an emergency. Make a list of the equipment and supplies, which should be present, and store it in the box or on the outside of the bag.

If supplies are removed or used in the emergency kit, replace them as soon as possible. Batteries, which are old, or other supplies, which can expire, should be replaced as required.

Items in your emergency kit like flashlights and radios should be tested regularly (rule of thumb – at least every six months) to ensure they are functioning properly. Any batteries stored in these units should be checked at the same time, to ensure they are not leaking or corroding. Alternately, remove and store batteries separately, but in the same location, to preserve battery life.

Food supplies

 **Non-perishable food supplies** sufficient for at least three days, preferably a week, for all members of your family who normally live in the home. In remote areas, think about stocking more food, based on your needs, location and circumstances.

Consideration should be given to the fact that limited or no power and limited heating sources may be present. Limited water sources could also be available throughout the emergency. Choose food that your family can and will eat, based on their particular tastes or special needs.

Items of this nature can include but not be limited to:

◉ **Canned meat, fish, poultry or meat spreads** which require no preparation

◉ **Canned soups, canned stews, and baked beans** (preferably the "ready-to-eat" variety as opposed to concentrated or condensed varieties, if limited water is available)

◉ **Canned fruits** and vegetables

◉ **Peanut butter**, honey, jams or jellies

◉ **Nuts** (unless allergic to these items)

◉ **Dried fruit**

◉ **Crackers**, cookies, or dry bread products (eg. melba toast)

◉ **Protein or fruit bars**

◉ **Canned milk, juices in cans or tetrapaks**, soft drinks and/or energy drinks in bottles (eg. GatorAde or PowerAde)

◉ **Instant packaged soups**, chicken, beef, or vegetable bouillon cubes or packcts

◉ **Packaged instant meals** (eg. cup- o'-noodles, instant pasta dishes, macaroni and cheese)

◉ **Juice powders**, powdered energy drink mixes (eg. GatorAde)

- **Spaghetti** or other dried pasta

- **Non perishable infant foods** (if young children are in the house)

- **Vitamins**

- **Non-perishable pet foods**

Packaged non-perishable food supplies which are self heating and require limited preparation are also available from various camping supply outlets, and may be purchased to supplement other stored food supplies in an emergency.

Emergency food supplies do not have to be obtained all at once, if you are on a tight budget. Purchasing a few items at a time, during normal grocery shopping trips over a few months can facilitate creating a stockpile of food. (See the "Stockpile Resources" section for a suggested way of stockpiling both food and other resources).

To determine if you have sufficient emergency food supplies, take out the supplies you have, and plan some meals, based on the number of people in your household and the number of days food supplies you wish to have on hand. Obtain and maintain additional food stocks, if you feel that the supplies you have are insufficient.

Ensure supplies of non-perishable foods are used and replaced on a regular basis (rule of thumb – at least every six to eight months), as even these types of foods can become stale with time.

Water supplies

 Water supplies are essential for human survival. While the human body can go without food for a number of days, a minimum of one gallon (4-4.5 litres) of water is required for drinking, cleaning and cooking purposes for an average adult per day. Store extra water for your pets as well. Additional water may be required for children, nursing mothers, sick or elderly individuals, especially in a hot environment.

During an emergency that occurs in an undamaged home in an urban area, sufficient water should still remain in the piping and water tank for several days, if used frugally (typical hot water tanks contain between 30-40 gallons of water). Water present in the hot water tank may be drained from the valve present at the bottom of the tank.

NOTE:

If water is being drained from the hot water tank, turn the gas or electric heating to the tank off prior to draining and let the tank cool, to ensure the tank does not overheat and cause a fire.

Water in the pipes may be drained by turning on a faucet present at the highest level of the house to release pressure (catch any water which may be released under pressure in a wash basin, bathtub, or clean storage containers). The remaining water may then be drained out from a faucet present in the lowest level of the home, into a washbasin, bathtub or clean storage containers.

During an emergency in winter where heating is not present in the house, water should be drained into containers for storage and use, as pipes containing water could freeze and burst.

Ice cubes stored in a freezer may also be used as an additional source of water.

In urban areas connected to city or town water, consider storing at least three days of extra water supplies for every person in the house, in the event that the water supply is cut off. Consider storing at least a week's supply of water in areas with limited water service.

> *NOTE:*
>
> *<u>DO NOT</u> use water in the <u>toilet</u> as a cleaning or drinking water source in an emergency, as it could contain bacterial contamination.*
>
> *<u>DO NOT</u> use water in a <u>waterbed</u> as a source of cleaning or drinking water, as pesticide based chemicals may be present in the casing of the bed or chemicals may have been added to the water to prevent the growth of algae, fungi or bacteria.*
>
> *<u>DO NOT</u> use water drained from a <u>water based heating system</u> in the home as a source of drinking water, as corrosion inhibitors or other chemicals may have been added to the water in the piping.*

Extra supplies of water may be stored for emergency use in clean empty food grade plastic containers, (eg. plastic milk jugs, and plastic drink containers) or empty and well rinsed bleach containers. Label these types of containers, to ensure they can be properly identified in an emergency. Change the water stored every six months.

If a severe weather warning is announced, with potential for cutting off utility services, consider storing additional water in empty, clean food grade containers, similar to those described above, or in pots and other cooking vessels. Clean bathtubs and washbasins may also be filled with water and used as a water reserve, as an additional preparedness measure.

NOTE:

<u>DO NOT</u> store water supplies in containers which have contained toxic chemicals or have been contaminated in some other manner.

<u>DO NOT</u> drink from an open container of water which is present near shattered glass or a broken mirror as shards or slivers of glass may be present in the water.

If you need to use outside sources of water in an emergency, the following sources may be considered:

- **Rainwater** (place clean open containers out in a rainstorm to collect the precipitation)

- **Uncontaminated streams**, rivers, or other moving bodies of water

- **Uncontaminated ponds** and lakes

- **Natural springs** or wells

Water treatment

All water collected from outside sources used for drinking, food preparation or hygiene should be treated prior to use, as it may contain microorganisms, which can cause diarrhea, dysentery, hepatitis, typhoid or other diseases. Salts, sediment, heavy metals and other chemicals may also be present in untreated water.

No treatment method is perfect in removing all forms of contamination. During an emergency where contaminated water may be involved, listen to local radio reports, and follow any specific instructions related to water treatment issued by local health or water resource officials in your area.

If no specific instructions have been issued by a government agency, the following treatments are most common and one or more of the following treatment methods may be used together or separately in an emergency:

Filtering or straining water through layers of paper towel or clean cloth can be used to remove suspended particles. Alternately, allow water to sit and let particles settle to the bottom.

Boiling your water supply will kill most microorganisms and is the safest method of treatment if heat is available during the emergency. The water should be brought to a roiling boil for 5-10 minutes, and then allowed to cool before drinking.

The taste of boiled drinking water may be improved by pouring it back and forth between two clean containers, to add oxygen back into the water, or by using the water to make beverages such as teas, coffee, or by mixing with powdered drink mixes.

Water disinfectants containing chlorine may also be used to kill microorganisms. The disinfectant most commonly available in a home is regular basic liquid bleach (5.25% Sodium Hypochlorite).

For clear water, use 1.5 drops of bleach per litre (6 drops per gallon), stir and let stand for 30 minutes prior to use. If the water does not have a slight chlorine taste, repeat the treatment and let stand for 15 minutes.

For cloudy water, use 4 drops of bleach per litre (16 drops per gallon) and let stand for 30 minutes. If water does not have a slight chlorine taste, repeat treatment, and let stand for 15 minutes.

NOTE:

DO NOT *use bleaches which contain scents; colour safe bleaches, or bleaches with other soap additives, for water purification purposes.*

Water purification tablets are also available commercially, which may be used as an alternate to the disinfection procedures listed above. If these types of tablets are to be used, follow the instructions outlined on the package, based on the volume of water to be treated.

As an advanced method of treatment, **distillation** may be used to remove additional microbes, heavy metals and other contaminants.

Heating and fuel supplies

Supplies of firewood which are stored in a readily available location around your home in the winter may be of use if an emergency cuts off your furnace, and you have a fireplace or wood stove installed in your home.

Extra supplies of propane, stored in a separate tank of appropriate size, may provide an additional source of fuel for cooking on a barbeque or other equipment, if your primary source of fuel to the home is cut off in an emergency.

First aid supplies

 A **first aid kit** may be required to assist in the treatment of minor injuries and to sustain more seriously injured persons prior to the arrival of trained medical staff and resources.

Typical items present in a basic first aid kit for a home include:

- **Adhesive sterile bandages** of various sizes

- **4-6 sterile gauze pads** (2 inch, 4 inch)

- **2-3 triangular sterile triangular cloth bandages**

- **2-3 rolls sterile roll bandages** (2 inch, 3 inch)
- **Fabric adhesive tape**
- **Pre-moistened antiseptic towelettes**
- **Scissors**
- **Tweezers**
- **Rubbing alcohol**
- **Soap**
- **First aid manual** or handbook
- **Fasteners** such as safety pins
- **Pain relieving medications** such as Aspirin, Tylenol, Advil, etc.

Additional items, which you may wish to include in your first aid kit:

- **Antibiotic ointment**
- **Tube of petroleum jelly** or other lubricant
- **Cotton swabs** (eg. Q-tips)
- **Thermometer**
- **Medicine dropper**
- **Needle and thread**
- **Latex gloves**
- **Antacid tablets** (for upset stomach)
- **Anti-diarrhea medication**
- **Anti-nausea medication** (eg. Gravol)
- **Laxative medication**

Items described above may be purchased separately, and stored in a marked storage box, or may be purchased in kit form from various hardware, safety supply, camping supply or retail outlets in your community.

For all family members living in the house, consider placing information related to their blood type, allergies to drugs and required medications on a card stored in the first aid kit and in the family medicine cabinet, for reference purposes. Ensure this information is updated as required, and that all family members know where the information is located.

Ensure that at least a week's supply of life sustaining medication is available in the house at all times, for every family member that requires them. Order additional medications before a week's supply is reached.

For family members with severe allergies, maintain a supply of appropriate allergy medications at all times. Renew and replace these medications before their expiry date.

Fire protection equipment

Fire protection equipment present in the house may be used to alert you to a problem and to extinguish a minor localized fire or limit a fire from spreading.

NOTE:

<u>DO NOT</u> attempt to extinguish a major fire, which has spread throughout the home using your own resources, as severe injuries, burns or fatalities may result.
Exit the home with your family, and phone your local fire department IMMEDIATELY!

Smoke detectors should be present on every level of your home, and should be checked regularly (rule of thumb – at least every six months), to ensure they are working properly. Replace batteries present in the detector as required, and replace the detector if it is found to be malfunctioning.

Fire safes may be purchased to store important records and valuables in the home, to protect against high heat conditions.

Fire extinguishers stored in the home, on the farm, or at the cottage can be used to fight minor fires.

Fires are generally classified by fire organizations as Type "A" (wood, fabric, paper, garbage, debris fires), Class "B" (flammable liquids, oil and grease fires) and Class "C" (electrical, wiring and appliance fires). The appropriate extinguisher needs to be available to fight the appropriate fire.

It is suggested that at least one fire extinguisher should be purchased for the home. The best type of extinguisher for this use would be a multipurpose, dry chemical variety (normally referred to as type "**ABC**", as it is suitable for use with all types of fires). The fire extinguisher should be certified by a recognized quality standards organization in your country (eg. Underwriter's Laboratories (UL).

Each fire extinguisher comes with hardware to allow the extinguisher to be mounted on a wall, to protect it from damage. Extinguishers should be mounted at a height of between 1 metre (approx. 3 feet) and 1.5 metres (approx. 5 feet) above the ground, to allow easy access by all members of the family trained in its use. It should also be placed in a location that is easily available to all family members, and may be placed close to areas of high fire risk.

Some suggested locations for fire extinguisher placement in a home include:

- **Near kitchen areas**, where oil and grease fires may occur
- **In workshops**
- **In a garage**
- **In a central location** such as a broom closet
- **In a laundry room**

Dry chemical or carbon dioxide extinguishers are pressurized and need to be recharged after being used in an actual fire, or if discharged for practice use. Extinguishers should be checked on a regular basis (rule of thumb, at least annually) even if they are not used, to ensure they are still charged.

Rechargeable fire extinguishers may be refilled at safety supply, farm supply and hardware stores in your local area, which provide this service (consult your local telephone directory for appropriate locations in your area).

Most fire extinguishers for the home are simple to operate and use. Ensure that your family is familiar with the location and operation procedures for the fire extinguishers stored in your home.

Other items, which may be used to extinguish a small non-electrical fire, include:

- A **wet mop** or broom

- A **garden hose** and nozzle

- **Buckets of water or sand**

- **Water soaked mats** or small rugs

- **Baking soda** (grease fires in a pan)

Other emergency preparedness items

Consider having at least one basic telephone in the home (eg. one telephone connected to a landline, which is not a cordless or other phone which requires additional power). Basic phones draw power directly from the phone line, and do not require a separate power connection. In a power failure, these types of phones may still be functional, allowing you to call for assistance.
Having a cellular phone can also be of great assistance in an emergency. However, it should be noted that cellular transmission towers may not be functional in a power failure, making cellular communication impossible.

Money and/or change should be kept in the house. Ensure you have a sufficient amount on hand to purchase needed supplies for a few days, based on your personal needs.
In the event of a major emergency, which knocks out power, banks and banking machines may not be available for an extended period of time.

Surge protectors and back-up power supplies may be placed on computers and electrical equipment, such as televisions and stereo equipment, to limit the possibility of damage from electrical surges and power  blackouts, resulting from an emergency. Backup power supplies provide limited power for a short period of time after a power outage (five to ten minutes). This will allow sensitive equipment such as computers, or audio and video electronic equipment, to be shut down normally, to prevent damage or loss of data.

Alternative power supplies such as small portable generators, portable rechargeable battery packs and solar panel solutions are also available on the market, for individuals with critical needs to maintain power during an outage.

An emergency generator can be used as an alternative power source, but it can be quite expensive to purchase, and continued maintenance is required, based on manufacturer's requirements, to ensure it is in good working order. The generator must also be run on a regular basis, to ensure it remains operational for use in an emergency.

Flood protection equipment is recommended in homes with basements to prevent or limit flooding in a heavy rainstorm.

 ⊚ **A check valve** placed in your sewer trap can limit the possibility of backup of sewage and water into your basement. This type of device is relatively inexpensive, and can prevent damage to items stored in your basement

The check valve allows water to flow down into the sewer, but has a ball present in the valve, which presses up against the inlet, if the sewer is filled or overflows. It should be noted that a check valve is not a perfect solution, as extremely high backpressure can cause the valve to fail, allowing flooding to still occur.

Check valves in a sewer trap will also not prevent seepage occurring from wide spread flooding. In a major flood, water can seep in through window wells and other openings in the house.

⊙ A **sump pump** may also be purchased and installed in a sump to control rising water coming from weeping tiles or a sewer. Pumps of this nature are normally configured to pump water to the outside of the home, and may operate automatically, or need to be powered manually, depending on the model purchased

These pumps can be expensive, based on their capacity and the head pressure required to pump the water from the basement to the outside of the home. If power is unavailable in the home in an emergency, the pump will also be inactive.

Like check valves, sump pumps will also not prevent wide spread flooding from occurring. Water can seep in through window wells and other openings in the house, making the pumping of water to the outside ineffective unless a dyke is present around the house.

Emergency information

Someone once said that information is power. This is especially true when it comes to emergency preparedness in the home. Information may save a life, or protect you from personal harm.

 **First aid**

There are a number of possibilities available to help you acquire useful medical information to assist you in an emergency.

- **Take a course in first aid and/or cardiopulmonary resuscitation (CPR)**, to teach you what can be done in a medical emergency, an accident or any emergency where injuries are involved

  Courses are available from the Red Cross, St. John's Ambulance and from other recognized organizations throughout the country (consult your local telephone directory for organizations in your area).

- **Obtain a first aid manual or handbook** from a recognized first aid organization, and store copies in your first aid kit, vehicle(s), backpack, and in other appropriate locations, based on the activities you normally undertake

 Phoning for help

- **Post emergency numbers** by your phone for easy access in an emergency

  In most urban areas, all emergency services provided by the city or town (police, fire, ambulance, etc.), may be accessed by dialing 9-1-1. Many rural municipalities and counties now provide this service as well. In addition, enhanced 9-1-1 service is also accessible via cellular phones in many areas.

  Consult your local phone directory to confirm procedures in your specific area.

  In addition to the emergency services number(s) in your community, you may wish to include additional

emergency numbers such as:

- **The emergency number for your local gas or other heating utility,** in the event of unexpected heating problems in your home
- **The emergency number for your local power company,** in the event of an emergency affecting power in your home
- **The emergency number for your local water or sewer utility** in the event of an emergency affecting water service in the home, or a water or sewer main break
- **The number for the nearest poison control centre** in your community, in the event of accidental poisoning
- **A number for contacting your family doctor**
- **Numbers for relatives** who may need to be contacted as the result of an emergency
- **An emergency number for obtaining life sustaining medications** on a priority basis, for persons in your family who have need of these types of medications
- **A number for obtaining emergency veterinary services** in your community, for pet emergencies after office hours, on weekends or holidays

⊚ **Post reminder information** by your phone

In an emergency situation when tension is high, we all have a tendency to become anxious and confused. Many people panic when phoning for help. These are natural reactions to an unusual and emotionally charged situation.

It is a psychological fact that persons in a high state of anxiety may have their minds "go blank", and may not remember important information such as their location, what has happened or the specifics of why they had phoned.

To assist in getting help when phoning to report an emergency, you may wish to post a reminder card by each phone in the house, which includes:

- **The telephone number** you are calling from
- The reminder **"Tell them who you are"**
- **The address of the house**, your town if outside a major urban centre, and a brief locator (eg. corner of Main Street and Fifth Avenue), or directions to get to the site if in a remote location
- The reminder **"Tell them what happened?"**
- The reminder **"Tell them what help is needed"**

A sample emergency contact and reminder list is presented in Figure 1.

 Contact points

⊚ If members of your family are away from home when an emergency occurs, and your home is damaged or destroyed, **establish one or two alternate locations where you will meet**, if required

---

⊙ **Establish a central communications point** with a relative, friend of the family or some other person, preferably in a location outside of the area which may be affected by the emergency, that family members can phone if separated (rule of thumb – try to pick a person at least 160 kilometres (100 miles) away, if possible

  • **If possible in a major emergency, have the person at your central communications point phone other out of area members of your family,** or other concerned individuals, to let them know you are alright. Telephone lines in the immediate area of the emergency will most likely be jammed, making it difficult or impossible to communicate directly

  • **Know the locations of your nearest fire, police and emergency medical facilities.** In a major emergency, communications services may be unavailable for an extended period of time

For younger children, place a card listing emergency contact information in a knapsack, jacket, or other appropriate location. Include information on the card such as your residence telephone number, address, business telephone numbers, alternate emergency meeting point, if the emergency occurs at home, and your alternate emergency telephone contact, to allow a responsible adult to contact your family if an emergency occurs which affects your child.

A sample emergency contact card is presented in Figure 2.

Emergency Contact List

Emergency Agencies	
Police	9-1-1 or
Fire	9-1-1 or
Ambulance	9-1-1 or
Poison Center	

Utilities		
Type	**Name**	**Emergency Number**
Heating		
Electricity		
Water		

Other		
Doctor		
Pharmacy (24 hr)		
Emergency Animal Hospital		

Emergency Contacts – Family (or Friends)		
Name	**Location**	**Telephone Number**

Emergency Contact Card

My Name Is	
My Home Address Is	
My Home Telephone Is	

If an emergency occurs while I'm away from home, please phone:		
Parents		**Telephone**
Mother's Name		
Father's Name		

If my parents can't be contacted, please phone:		
Name	Address	Telephone

If an emergency occurs at home, my parents want me to meet them at:	
Location	
Address	

Figure 1
Sample Emergency Contact and Reminder list

• •

I'm phoning from _____ and my name is (tell them your name)
(Telephone number)

We require assistance at: _____ in _____
(Address)   *(City or town)*

Put a quick description of how to get to the location here
(eg. it's a bungalow at the corner 1ˢᵗ Avenue and Main Street)

Tell them what happened *(Reminder)*

Tell them what type of help you need? *(Eg. medical, police, fire ambulance) (Reminder)*

> **NOTE:**
>
> *Fill in the appropriate telephone number, address, town and location information for the home where the information will be posted, to ensure it is easy to access in an emergency.*

Figure 2
Sample Emergency Contact for Children

• •

> **NOTE:**
>
> *Modify this card accordingly based on your personal situation or lifestyle.*

Insurance

We assume many things in our daily lives.

One of the most common assumptions is that insurance policies, which we obtain for our property, will cover all losses that could occur in an emergency. This may not necessarily be the case.

As an item of emergency preparedness, you should examine the risks, which you identified on your list (as discussed in the section "Where to Start?" at the beginning of the book). Bring the list and speak with your insurance agent, to determine if you are covered for all potential emergency situations which could occur.

Specific items which you should ask, depending on the risks you've identified may include, but not be limited to:

⊚ Does my insurance policy cover damage to my property **from all losses related to fire** (including forest fires, if applicable)? Are there any specific exclusions?

⊚ Does my insurance policy cover damage to my property **from all losses related to floods or flash floods?** Are there any specific exclusions?

⊚ Does my insurance policy cover damage to my property **from all losses related to wind damage, tornados or hurricanes?** Are there any specific exclusions?

⊚ Does my insurance policy cover damage to my property **from all losses related to earthquakes?** Are there any specific exclusions?

⊚ Does my insurance policy cover damage to my property **from all losses related to hail?** Are there any specific exclusions?

- Does my insurance policy cover **damage to electrical equipment related to major power surges or lightning strikes?** Are there any specific exclusions?

- Does my insurance policy cover damage to my property **from any losses related to a major power loss over an extended period?**

- Does my insurance policy cover **damage to all buildings, vehicles and contents?** Are there any specific exclusions?

Ask appropriate questions for every insurance policy which may be impacted by an emergency, including policies covering your home, cottages, road vehicles, boats or other property.

Depending on where you are located, and the risks which insurance companies have determined for the area, you may find that the answer to some of the questions above will be "no", or that exclusions apply. If so, you may wish to discuss whether additional coverage does exist, for items which may be excluded.

If no insurance is present for specific risks in your area, you may want to contact your local municipal, county, provincial, state or federal emergency preparedness offices, to determine if options exist for purchasing additional coverage through the government, or whether government programs would cover losses for items not covered by private insurance. In many cases, these types of options do exist, depending on the country you live in.

In some cases, such as apartments and condominiums, separate insurance policies are present, which cover the building and the interior contents as separate items. Contact your landlord or condominium association, and ask them the appropriate questions, noted above, to see whether any deficiencies in coverage or exclusions may exist.

As a suggestion keep a photocopy of your insurance policy(s) with your emergency kit, in a waterproof pouch, envelope or bag, for easy access if an emergency occurs. You may also want to store original copies of these documents in an off-site secure location, such as a safety deposit box in a bank, in the event of major damage to the home.

In addition, you may wish to prepare an inventory of valuable pieces in the house, including items like sofas, chairs, tables, beds, wall units, electronics, etc., complete with serial numbers, if applicable. Take pictures and provide descriptions, as required, for insurance purposes. Preferably, store this information in an off-site secure location like a safety deposit box, for ready reference purposes, if your home is damaged or destroyed.

If valuable documents and items cannot be stored off-site in a secure location, consider purchasing a fire safe, which can protect valuables against high heat conditions and other emergencies.

Examine the inventory on an annual basis, or update it as required, if items are bought, sold or given away.

Personal emergency plan

Emergency plans for corporations and cities can be extremely large and complex documents, sometimes thousands of pages in length. Personal emergency plans do not have to be large or complex.

Consider preparing a one page personal emergency plan, which can be posted in an easily accessible place or places in the home, and distributed, to responsible members of your family.

Typical information you may wish to include are items like:

⊚ **A floor plan of the home**, showing the location of exits in a fire, as well as the locations of your basic emergency kit, first aid kit and fire extinguisher(s)

⊚ **The primary location and an alternate location where you will meet** if your family must leave the home quickly and you become separated in a fire

⊚ **A contact number (friend or relative) that you all can phone**, either local or outside the impact area or both, if you can't reach the meeting point

⊚ **Safe places within your home** to go to in other potential emergencies, which affect your specific community (eg. in a hurricane, tornado, flood, etc.)

An example of a personal emergency plan is presented in Figure 3.

A more complex personal emergency plan can be created, as required, based on your special needs and requirements.

Additional information you may wish to add includes:

⊚ **Names of contact persons in a support network**, if one has been created to assist you in an emergency (See the "Special Needs" section for descriptions of what a support network is)

⊚ **Medical information**, including:

  • Your doctor's name

  • Medical conditions you suffer from

  • Medications you take, including dosage and frequency

  • Treatment(s) required and frequency

  • Operating instructions for critical life support equipment

Figure 3 – Personal Emergency Response Plan
(Example Only)

FACING STREET

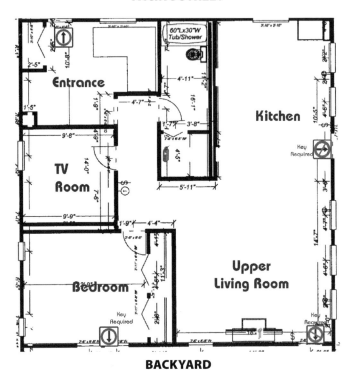

UPPER FLOOR

Open Emergency Exit

Exit – Key Required (Security Lock)

Flashlight

Fire Extinguisher

Primary Exit	Main Entrance Door – Upper Floor – Street Side
Secondary Exit	Bedroom – Upper Floor – Back Yard
Secondary Exit	Master Bedroom – Lower Floor – Back Yard

From corner of Highway #5 and Highway #43, go east on Highway #43 2 kilometres to Range Road 23. Turn right (south) and go south 3 kilometres to Township road #530. Turn left (east) and go 0.5 kilometres east. House has brown wooden siding and is located on the south side of the road.

Personal Emergency Plan (Example)
67 Anywhere Street

Emergency Kit
Emergency Food Supply

First Aid Kit

Emergency Water

Storm Shelter

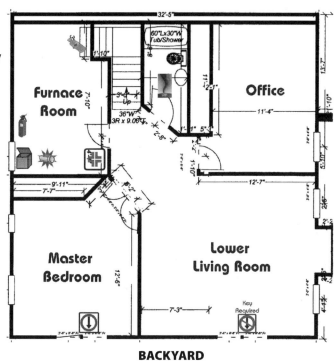

FACING STREET

Furnace Room

Office

Master Bedroom

Lower Living Room

BACKYARD

LOWER FLOOR

Emergency Contacts	
Police, Fire, Ambulance	9-1-1
John Smith (Brother) - Edmonton	780-555-1234
George Smith (Brother) - Vancouver	604-555-8923

Evacuation checklist

 In major emergency situations, various government agencies in your local area have the legal right to officially declare a state of emergency, which gives the appropriate agency the permission to exercise extraordinary powers to control the effects of the emergency. One of these powers, which may affect you personally, is the right to declare a mandatory evacuation of the affected area.

If you are required to evacuate your home, notification may come with extremely short notice and a short time frame. It is therefore wise to plan for this contingency as part of your emergency preparedness activities, as you may have to be away from your home for hours, or even a number of days or weeks, based on the severity of the situation.

An **evacuation checklist** does not have to be a complex document – it is merely a checklist or memory jogger, listing important items to take with you and important preparatory activities to undertake if you must leave your home quickly.

Some reminder items, which may be included on an evacuation checklist, include:

- **Taking your basic emergency kit** with you

- **Taking any prescription medicines** with you that you or your family require

- **Taking any necessary prescription glasses** with you

- **Taking any other special needs** required by your family (eg. special food requirements, dentures, special appliances or health monitors, etc.)

- ⊙ **Taking clothing for two to three days** for each family member, if possible (ensure at least one change of clothes per person)

- ⊙ **Taking blankets or sleeping bags** and pillows for each member of your family

- ⊙ **Taking spare money** with you

- ⊙ **Taking your pets** and pet food

- ⊙ **Taking keys to your vehicle**, your home and keys to other locations you are evacuating to if required

Keep your evacuation checklist in an accessible location, where it can be easily found in an emergency (eg. your home emergency kit).

As an additional item of evacuation preparedness, you may wish to determine which evacuation routes are available, if you must leave the area where your home is located quickly by vehicle or on foot. Determine what the primary route would be, and provide yourself with secondary routes, if available.

You may wish to add a description of the evacuation routes to your evacuation checklist, for easy reference.

Important documents

We all have important documents which are either irreplaceable, or are required for our personal or business needs.

These include:

- **Passports**
- **Property deeds**
- **Mortgages**
- **Wills**
- **Stock certificates, bonds or other negotiable financial documents**
- **Insurance documents**
- **Personal financial databases or records**

In a major emergency situation, these items can be damaged or destroyed, making them difficult or impossible to replace.

Emergency preparedness plans to protect documents can include:

- **Storing all important documents in one location**, so they can be moved or removed quickly if an emergency occurs

- **Storing <u>original</u> documents in a secure off-site location** such as a safety deposit box in a bank or other financial institution and keep <u>photocopies</u> of important documents present at home, for easy reference purposes

- **Storing important documents in your home in a fire safe**, or fire resistant container

- **Burning multiple copies of important software**, databases or electronic documents to CDs, and storing at least one copy of these CDs at an off-site location

- **Scanning copies of irreplaceable original photos or negatives to a CD**, so that copies can be made if required

- **Keeping records of valuable items for insurance purposes**, and storing a copy of these records at a secure, off-site location

All important records, copies or electronic documents and databases should be updated if changes have been made.

In addition, if you have a computer, consider backing-up important information contained on your computer hard drive to a CD or other appropriate media on a weekly basis, to prevent loss of information resulting from an emergency.

 Utilities

Normally, utility companies would shut down services, if required, in a localized emergency condition. However, in a major emergency with widespread impacts and damage, utility personnel may not be available to respond to individual concerns. As a safety precaution in an emergency you may need to shut off utilities in the home yourself, to prevent danger to yourself or your family.

Know where cut-off valves are for your gas, water and electrical services in the house. If needed, ensure that you have proper tools in your emergency kit to allow gas and/or water valves to be shut off in an appropriate manner.

As an added precaution, you could document the location of these switches or valves, and include this information on your emergency plan and store it in your home emergency kit.

Emergency pre-planning when building a home

In many cases, persons building their own homes choose locations known for scenic beauty or view, without consideration for what may happen in an emergency.

Your home may be required to meet certain required construction standards related to emergency preparedness by law, in the country, province, state, municipality, or local area you live in. If building a home yourself, check local regulatory and building permits and development standards, to ensure all necessary requirements are being met.

Floodplains are low lying areas, which will easily flood if water levels rise in an emergency. By building on a floodplain, usually near the bank of a river or stream, or right on an ocean beach, you may be subject to more severe emergency conditions if a flood or hurricane does occur. Consider building your home further back from the water, in an elevated area and off a floodplain if possible, to limit damage from tidal swells and rising floodwaters.

Cliff top or mountainside views can be spectacular, but homes built in these locations may be destroyed by landslides, unstable ground in an avalanche, heavy rainfall, flash flooding, or an earthquake. Find out about the soil stability in the area where you plan to construct, and determine whether any special construction considerations need to be implemented by law. Consider building with a sufficient buffer area between your home and the edge of cliffs or slide areas to minimize damage in an emergency.

In forested areas, assess what may happen if a forest fire occurs.

When designing your home for a forested area, consider use of fire resistant or non-combustible siding materials (eg. brick, stucco), where possible. Consider using fire resistant materials for roofing, including asphalt shingles, slate or clay tile, in place of easily ignited cedar or pine shakes. Consider using tempered glass for the outside windows, as it has a greater heat resistance than regular glass, and will not shatter as easily if exposed to higher heat. Shattered windows allow easy access for fires into your home.

When building your home, try to locate it away from the foot of a ridge or hillside. In a forest fire, fire can sweep down a ridge very quickly and engulf a home.

Consider having sufficient open ground between dense stands of trees and your home, to prevent easy access for a nearby fire. Clear slopes or ridges of deadfall, and older trees to at least 30 metres (100 feet) back from the home. Maintain at least a 10 metre (30 foot) clearance around your home at all times. Undertake maintenance regularly to keep the buffer area clear of trees and vegetation.

When designing your landscaping, consider spacing trees so that fire cannot easily spread from treetop to treetop, even as the tree matures. Also consider using plant, tree and brush species local to your area, which may be more fire resistant.

Place driveways, concrete sidewalks or gravel paths to act as a "fuel-break", in the event of a fire. Consider having ample turnaround space near your home, to allow easy movement of fire equipment, and clearly mark your driveway and access road.

In areas subject to **hurricanes, tornadoes, or other high wind conditions**, consider installing shutters, which can be quickly and securely closed, to safely protect windows from flying debris.

In developed areas, like a city or a town, near major highways or rail lines, near seaports or in rural areas, near an industrial facility or centre, determine what potential hazards may be present in the surrounding area, prior to purchasing the property.

If an airport is nearby, determine whether the area where you wish to build is on the flight path of one of the runways. In an emergency involving aircraft with mechanical difficulties, you may be impacted if an emergency landing is attempted.

Many people do not realize that in a major emergency involving a fire or release at a chemical or petroleum facility, a natural disaster affecting other industrial facilities, a train derailment, or a road accident involving dangerous gases may have an impact on your home, even if you are a significant distance away.

Releases of liquid chemicals or petroleum related products can also impact groundwater resources, potentially contaminating drinking water wells used by residents, especially if soil conditions are extremely permeable (eg. sand, gravel or soil in areas where water wells are extremely shallow).

Situating your new home well away from industrial facilities, major dangerous goods transport routes, rail lines, gasoline stations and storage locations for gases such as propane or ammonia, can significantly reduce the possibility of impact from chemical or petroleum related emergencies.

Maintenance or modification

As part of your emergency preparedness efforts, you may want to consider preventative measures, which can lessen the impact of an emergency.

In locations where major emergencies are frequent occurrences, specific maintenance procedures or home modifications may be required by law, to limit damage in an emergency. Check with the appropriate local municipal, state or provincial authorities to determine specific requirements for your area.

If no specific preventative measures are required in your local area, you may want to undertake some preventative maintenance or modification procedures yourself. These could include:

General maintenance for emergencies

⊚ **Have at least two ground level exits clear at all times** in the event you have to evacuate your home quickly

⊚ **Check hallways, stairwells, doorways, windows and other appropriate areas, to ensure they are kept clear at all times**. Remove or secure furniture to the wall, if it could be knocked over, blocking your way or tripping you in an emergency

⊚ **Consider keeping emergency lights with their own built-in power source plugged into power outlets in key areas**, to light your way if evacuation to a safer area is required. These lights will remain on if a power disruption occurs

- ⊙ **Keep a flashlight and hard soled footwear near your bed**, for easy access, if an emergency occurs at night

- ⊙ **Consider storing a tool which can easily break glass near a window**, if you must leave quickly in an emergency, and other exit means are limited

- ⊙ **If you have chosen to install a security deadbolt**, which requires a key to open it on both sides of the door, store an extra key in an accessible location near the interior side of the door, to allow the door to be opened quickly in an emergency. Ensure all members of your household know where this key is located

- ⊙ **Ensure that your house number is visible from the street in all seasons**. Cut back any vegetation or remove objects which may obscure the number in an emergency

 ## Maintenance for fires in the home

- ⊙ **Test your smoke detector(s)** at least once every six months. Replace batteries as necessary

- ⊙ **Check the gauge on each fire extinguisher** at least once per year to ensure it is still pressurized. Recharge it or replace disposable extinguishers if the gauge indicates low pressure

- ⊙ **Store flammable liquids properly** in and around the home

- ⊙ **Remove flammable materials** which are stored near areas with potential open ignition sources or heating elements

Maintenance for forest fires

- **Consider keeping a clearing of at least 10 metres (30 feet) around your home**, to allow access for fire fighting equipment in an emergency, or a greater distance, if required by local fire regulations in your area

- **Remove "ladder fuels" from around your home** (eg. dense large brush, dead tree branches closer to the ground), which can link grasses and treetops in a fire situation

- **Consider pruning tree limbs on large trees** so they are no lower than 2-3 metres (6-10 feet) above the ground

- **Maintain a "fuel break" around your home**, to prevent fires from easily and quickly approaching your home. Driveways, sidewalks and gravel paths around the home can limit the movement of ground fires

- **Mow grass regularly**, to limit the amount of fuel in a ground fire

- **Remove leaf clutter** from your roof, gutters or yard

- **Dispose of any debris and cuttings** in a proper manner, to limit supplies of fuel which may be ignited in a fire

- **Trim branches of trees**, which are overhanging your roof or chimney, to prevent fires from spreading from trees to flammable roof coverings (eg. wooden shingles)

- **Store stockpiles of firewood away from the home** or any other buildings

- **If you have a permanent in-ground sprinkler system,**

maintain it regularly, as it could assist in wetting down areas which may be impacted by a fire. Maintain household garden hoses in good condition, as they might be required in a fire related emergency

⊚ **Don't keep stockpiles of flammable materials under decks**, or by the side of a house

⊚ **Consider using trellises which are made of non-flammable materials** such as metal

⊚ **Cover vent holes in the roof or under eaves** with wire mesh no larger than 25mm (1/8″), to prevent hot sparks and cinders from easily entering the attic or other parts of the home

 ## Preparing for earthquakes

⊚ **Consider bolting pictures, mirrors, cabinets, book cases and other heavy objects to wall studs**, so they will not easily fall off or topple

⊚ **Consider placing heavy wall hangings (eg. pictures, mirrors, sconces, lighting fixtures) away from places where a person may be sitting or lying**, such as a sofa or bed

⊚ **Consider bracing, reinforcing or securing overhead light fixtures** to prevent them from easily falling

⊚ **Consider nailing a strip of wood to the front edge of book shelves,** to prevent books from easily falling off the shelf

⊚ **Consider placing latches on cabinet doors**, to prevent contents from spilling out

- **Fasten open shelf brackets to studs in the wall,** and attach the shelf directly to the bracket

- **Place large or heavy objects on lower shelves**

- **Store breakable items such as glass bottles or china in low cabinets,** which can be latched or secured to minimize the possibility of doors opening unexpectedly

- **Consider strapping water heaters and other large appliances to wall studs** using strap iron (sometimes called plumbers tape), and/or bolting them to the floor

- **Store flammable liquids, pesticides and other chemicals on lower shelves** in secure cabinets

- **Consider using Velcro type taping** to secure lighter objects to sturdier objects

 ## Hurricanes or windstorms

- **Consider installing shutters** which can be quickly and securely closed to safely protect windows from flying debris

 ## Maintenance for blizzards or ice storms

- **Check alternate heating sources which may be in your home** (eg. fireplaces, wood stoves, kerosene heaters) to ensure they are working properly, prior to cold weather occurring

- **Have chimneys and flues checked professionally each year**, and cleaned as necessary

- **Have a stockpile of fuel for your alternate heating source available at all times**, during the cold weather months, sufficient for three full days to a week of use

- **Consider installing a smoke detector and carbon monoxide detector** in an appropriate location near the area to be heated by the alternate heating source. Site these detectors carefully, according to manufacturers instructions, as siting detectors too close to the heating source may cause the detector(s) to give false alarms constantly during normal operation of the heating source

- **Consider adding additional insulation to your home**, replacing weather stripping that is damaged, and adding energy efficient or thermal pane storm windows to your home, if not already present. These items can increase the time that your home will retain heat, if a heating disruption does occur

- **Insulate water lines near exterior walls**, if not done already, as they will be less likely to freeze if heating is cut off

In an actual emergency in the home

 If a medical emergency occurs ....

⊚ **In a life threatening emergency situation,** phone
the local emergency number in your community (9-1-
1 or other specific number for your community), and
request medical assistance immediately, as time
may be critical. Give them the following important
information:

- **Your name** and the phone number where you
  are located
- **The address of the home** and a brief description
  of where it is located (eg. corner of ____ Street
  and ____ Avenue).
- **Tell them what happened**
- **Tell them what type of help you need** (eg.
  medical and ambulance assistance)

Ensure the door to the house is unlocked to allow
emergency personnel to access the residence, if you are
administering first aid, CPR or other potentially life
saving procedures.

⊚ **Provide first aid** to the injured individual or person in
distress based on their particular needs

Priority first aid measures include:

- **Ensuring the victim is breathing,** and that
  their heart is functioning

- **Administering appropriate cardiopulmonary resuscitation procedures**, if the person has stopped breathing or their heart has stopped

- **Controlling external bleeding**, especially for large deep wounds

- **Looking for signs of internal bleeding**, and administering appropriate first aid procedures

- **Treating shock**, if it occurs as a result of injuries

- **Keeping the victim warm**, and as comfortable as possible

- **Checking for signs of other potential severe medical concerns**, and administering appropriate first aid treatment

- **Treating minor, non-life threatening conditions** in an appropriate manner

NOTE:

Consult with an emergency medical professional or refer to a first aid handbook from a recognized first aid organization for specific procedures, if you are unclear as to what must be done. Also, remember that taking first aid and CPR training can save a life!

⊚ **Provide additional support** to the injured person as required

⊚ **Monitor injured or ill persons on a regular basis**, to ensure their condition remains stable. Provide additional first aid treatment or care, as necessary

- **Assist emergency medical personnel** as required, if directed to do so in a life threatening medical emergency

- **In non life threatening situations where additional care may be required**, assist in transporting the person to appropriate facilities, such as an emergency medical facility in a hospital, a walk-in clinic or their doctor for additional treatment or care, based on the nature or severity of the medical emergency

- **For minor situations where no additional outside care is required**, assist the person who is injured or ill, as required

NOTE:

If the nature or severity of the injury or illness is unusual or unclear, or a minor illness or injury is causing increasing distress or pain to an individual, consider erring on the side of caution and seek medical advice or assistance <u>*immediately.*</u>

Better to be safe than sorry!

 If a power disruption occurs ....

- **Get your flashlight(s) if the home is in darkness**, to assist you in safely maneuvering around the home

- **Turn off appliances and electronics** in use at the

time of the power outage, to prevent damage when the power returns, and to help your power provider to restore regular power

- **Extreme power surges can occur** as a result of reactivation of all active equipment on the power grid at the same time. This can result in additional power shutdowns or brownouts, which lengthen the time required to restore normal power service

- **Equipment, like computers, which are connected to a battery backup** and do not shut down automatically, should be shut down immediately to prevent damage or loss of data

◉ **Consider turning off power switches** on power bars and surge protectors, to limit the possibility of start-up surges damaging sensitive equipment

◉ **Use alternative lighting sources** to light your home:

- **Battery powered lights** are safest, and can provide steady bright lighting while battery power supplies last

- **Alternative power supply flashlights or lamps,** which do not use batteries (See New Age Emergency Preparedness), can also be used to provide safe lighting for limited periods in an emergency. However, they require recharging on a regular basis, using a built in dynamo, shaking or other methods

- **Emergency light sticks,** which contain chemicals that provide safe lighting when shaken or bent, can supply lighting for a number of hours in an emergency. These lighting sources can only be used once in an emergency, and then must be disposed of

- **Candles** are readily available in most households and can provide a steady source of light in still air conditions, but may gutter and burn unevenly if air currents are present. They may also provide limited, flickering lighting, which may be of poor quality for reading and other activities. Care should be taken, as knocking over the open flame of a candle can ignite a fire if flammable materials are nearby

- **Oil or paraffin lamps** have become popular for use in households, in place of candles, and have many of the same properties as described above for candles. Care should also be taken with these items, as knocking over the open flame of an oil lamp can ignite a fire if flammable materials are nearby

- **Kerosene or liquid fuel camping lanterns** can provide bright steady reliable sources of light, while fuel supplies last. Care should be taken using these lamps, as a lamp, which is knocked over, can break, spilling fuel and potentially igniting a fire. **ADEQUATE VENTILATION MUST BE PRESENT AT ALL TIMES** in the area where the lantern(s) is in operation, to prevent buildup of carbon monoxide, or other flammable or toxic gases

- **Emergency lighting sources** such as wick lamps can be fabricated if no other lighting is available, using kitchen type vegetable oils, a clean glass jar free of labels, and some cotton string or other wick material. The light generated from these sources is generally limited and of poor quality. Care should be taken with these items, as knocking over the wick lamp can ignite a fire

NOTE:

Do not use kerosene, gasoline or diesel fuel in a wick lamp constructed for emergency purposes, as vapours from these materials can start a fire. Use only kitchen based vegetable type oils for this purpose.

- **Reflectors** made of aluminum foil or mirrors can also be used with lighting sources to increase and concentrate the available light from an emergency lighting source. Placing emergency lighting on a white surface will also increase reflection, making lighting seem brighter

If power is out for an extended period of time:

- **Use available lighting sources on an intermittent basis** to conserve and extend limited battery power or fuel supplies. If fuel or battery supplies have reached critically low levels, use lighting sources only when absolutely necessary

- **If you have a backup generator available**, use this to provide critical power needs (heating, lighting, cooking, etc.) as required. If fuel supplies for the generator have reached critically low levels, use generator power on an intermittent basis and only as absolutely necessary

- **Consider using available food in the house** in the following order of priority:
  - **Use perishable foods** in your refrigerator or other locations first, if possible. Foods which require preparation may be cooked on a barbecue or camp style stove, if available. If no cooking facilities are available, consider

using up food supplies which do not require preparation first (eg. fresh vegetables, fresh fruits, spreads and jams, milk or other perishable liquid foods

- **Use food from your freezer** next. Freezers, that are well insulated and filled with food, can keep items well frozen for two to three days, if the freezer is not opened continuously. If no cooking facilities are available, consider using up food supplies, which do not require preparation (eg. frozen bread, frozen packaged goods, frozen desserts, etc.)

NOTE:

Food such as meat, poultry, or vegetables in a freezer, which has thawed and cannot be used immediately should be thrown out to prevent the possibility of bacterial contamination.

WHEN IN DOUBT THROW IT OUT!

- **Use non-perishable foods** next, or to supplement foods listed above

 If a heating disruption occurs ....

- **If a gas supply has been disrupted or stopped temporarily** shut off the gas valve into the house to prevent the possibility of an explosion when gas service is restored

NOTE:

If the smell of gas is present in your home, evacuate the home and contact your local fire department <u>immediately.</u>

⊙ **Attempt to conserve heat,** which is already present in your home, for as long as possible. Cover areas in your home where cold can easily enter with materials such as plastic sheeting or curtains, extra bed sheets, or other available coverings

⊙ **If required, exit the home through an enclosed location** such as a garage or other space with more than one door, instead of a door which opens directly to the outside, to limit the amount of heat which could escape directly from the home

⊙ **As temperatures drop, for extended heating disruptions**, consider moving into an enclosed room (eg. a room with walls and a door or doors) preferably in the centre of the home, to increase the amount of surrounding insulation. Close doors to conserve heat as much as possible

⊙ **Consider using alternative heating sources**, if they are available:

  • **Electric space heaters** may be used to heat a smaller area, if a heating disruption has occurred but electrical power is still available. Extreme care should be taken to ensure that open heating elements cannot ignite flammable materials and cause a fire

- **Fireplaces or wood stoves** can provide adequate heating in a room, if they are available. However, sufficient fuel must be easily obtainable throughout the heating disruption to keep a fire going. Wood burning fireplaces or stoves also require proper ventilation to ensure an adequate burn, and to prevent build-up of carbon monoxide or other toxic gases in the home

- **Liquid fueled camp lanterns** can provide localized heating in a small area. However, sufficient fuel must be present in order to successfully operate equipment of this nature. In addition, adequate ventilation is required to allow this equipment to be safely operated, to prevent build-up of carbon monoxide, or other toxic gases

- **Lighting sources such as candles and oil lamps** can provide limited localized heating in a small area. Care should be taken, as knocking over the open flame of a candle or oil lamp can ignite a fire if flammable materials are nearby

If alternate heating sources are available during the heating disruption, consider heating one enclosed room only to conserve limited fuel supplies. Ensure adequate ventilation is present, based on the type of heating source used.

- **For heating disruptions where the temperature may go below the freezing point of water**, consider draining water lines and the water tank in the home, to prevent water pipes and equipment from bursting as water freezes. Clean water supplies should be stored and saved for drinking and cleaning purposes throughout the emergency

- **Wear additional clothing sufficient to remain warm**, but do not overly dress, as perspiration will make clothing damp, causing it to lose its insulative properties. Perspiration, which evaporates, can take away valuable heat and chill your body. Feet are especially prone to perspiration, and should be kept as warm and dry as possible

- **Dress in several layers of lighter clothing**, and add or remove layers, as required. The whole body, and especially the torso, must remain warm to maintain circulation to the head, hands, and feet. Poor blood flow results in little heat to the extremities. Wear gloves, shoes, and a hat, if temperatures drop, to prevent heat from dissipating easily from your body

- **Remember to eat regularly to maintain your energy**, even if the food is cold. The body needs food to maintain heat

- **Huddle with others under a blanket or other covering** as two or more bodies can provide better warmth than one. A bed can be the warmest place in a heating disruption, if sufficient covers are available. Huddling with pets can also be a source of additional warmth

- If the heating disruption is localized and is expected to be of extended duration, consider moving to another location, where heat is still available, such as a friend's or relative's home. In a major emergency, which disrupts heating for an extended period, consider moving to a government organized heated shelter until heating is restored

- Follow appropriate advice given in other sections, related to water, power outages and other emergencies, as required

- For gas powered heating, once service is restored, do not attempt to restart the furnace or turn gas service back on yourself, as serious injury or a fatality can result from improper service procedures. Wait until a qualified service representative can restore heating in a safe manner

 ## If water supply is disrupted or contaminated...

- If water or sewer pipes have broken in an emergency and there is potential for contamination, shut off the water valve into the house to prevent contaminated water from entering the home

- If the water supply disruption is localized and is expected to be of extended duration, consider moving, temporarily, to another location where normal water service is still available, such as a friend's or relative's home. In a major emergency which disrupts water service for an extended period, consider moving to a government organized shelter until services are restored

Water management

⊙ **Use stored water supplies, or water supplies present in various locations in the home** as required throughout the emergency (See the Water Supplies section under Supplies and Equipment above). For water outages of extended duration, attempt to conserve water supplies as much as possible

Consider the following priorities for water use in an emergency, based on the amount of water available:

- **Use sufficient water for drinking and cleaning,** based on the number of family members in the home. As a rule of thumb, approximately one gallon (4.5 litres of water) is required per day for an adult family member for drinking and personal hygiene purposes, if used frugally. While humans can survive without food for several days, drinking water is an essential part of survival in an emergency

- **Conserve water used for cooking purposes,** if possible. Juices and water present in canned vegetables may also be used to supplement water supplies for cooking purposes. Store these water supplies in clean containers and recycle them for cooking uses during the emergency if practical and feasible

- **Use water for other purposes** only on a critical, as needed basis

⊙ **If supplies of water within the home run low,** consider seeking additional water supplies from outside sources described previously, and treat them appropriately prior to use (See the Water Supplies section under Supplies and Equipment above)

Government agencies will attempt to provide alternative clean water sources in a major emergency, but it should be noted that these water supplies might be finite in nature, until normal service is restored. Only take sufficient water to serve you or your family's needs on an emergency basis, until normal supply is restored. Remember that in a critical water shortage, water supplies must also serve all other members of your community as well.

Keeping clean

◉ **Discard dirty water, which has been used for personal cleaning purposes**. If water for cleaning runs low, consider the following temporary substitutes to remove dirt from skin:

- Prepackaged moist towelettes
- Rubbing alcohol (isopropyl alcohol)
- Lotions containing alcohol
- Antibacterial hand washes
- Other waterless hand cleaners
- Face creams, and hand lotions

With limited cleaning supplies, concentrate on keeping hands clean, as anything touched can carry disease. Hands should be washed prior to handling food and drinking water, after caring for the sick, and especially after going to the toilet.

◉ **If limited water is available for washing hair**, use a stiff hairbrush to comb out hair and keep it clean longer

- **Use baking soda** as a substitute for toothpaste to keep teeth clean

- **If sufficient water is available, and you wish to disinfect items** which may be contaminated with germs or bacteria, use a solution of 250 ml of bleach to 22.5 L (one cup of bleach to 5 gallons) water

Managing sewage

Without water, toilets will not be functional, making use of normal toilet facilities difficult at best. Leaving urine and feces in a non-functional toilet for an extended period in an emergency, can lead to potential concerns related to disease and insects, as well as aesthetic concerns related to odour.

- **A temporary toilet can be created** using a large pail with a tight lid, and a chair with a hole cut in the center of a seat, or a wooden box with a hole cut out, and a toilet seat. When not in use, the pail should be tightly covered. If the temporary toilet is not in an enclosed area, hang an old shower curtain, or some other temporary curtain around the toilet for privacy, if possible

- **In urban areas in an emergency**, accumulated wastes from a temporary toilet may be disposed of directly to the outdoor septic sewer access or manhole on a temporary basis. In rural areas, accumulated wastes may be disposed of to a septic tank through a pump out access, on a temporary basis

NOTE:

Do __not__ dispose of wastes down a __storm sewer access__, as most storm sewers are not connected to a waste treatment facility, and untreated wastes may flow directly into a river or other watercourse.

- **If disposal methods described above are unavailable**, human wastes may be buried under 30 to 60 centimetres (12 to 24 inches) of dirt, as a temporary disposal method

NOTE:

Do __not__ dispose of solid or liquid human wastes __on the surface of the ground__, as insects or rodents can pick up disease germs and transmit them to other species or to humans.

- **Control odour and insect concerns for a temporary toilet** by sprinkling lime or household bleach in the toilet. After the emergency is over, thoroughly clean and sanitize the pail used as a temporary toilet, or dispose of it appropriately, to prevent disease

- **Follow appropriate advice given in other sections** as required, related to heating, power outages and other emergencies

If a fire is occurring in the home...

⊙ **Alert everyone in the home** that a fire has occurred by yelling **FIRE**!

⊙ **If the fire is small**, attempt to put it out using a fire extinguisher

NOTE:

Do __not__ attempt to extinguish a major fire, which has spread throughout the home, using your own resources, as severe injuries, burns or fatalities may result.

Exit the home with your family, and phone your local fire department immediately!

⊙ **If attempting to leave a closed room in a fire**, feel the door as high as you can reach. **IF THE DOOR IS HOT, DO NOT OPEN IT** as fire may be directly present on the other side. Seek another means of escape from the room

NOTE:

SUPERHEATED AIR can rush into a room if the door is opened, which can be fatal if inhaled.

⊙ **If the door is NOT hot**, still take care, as the doorknob could be hot enough to burn you. Open the door slightly and with care, with your face turned away, to protect your lungs in the event that superheated air or smoke enters the room

Feel the air to see if it is hot. If so, close the door and seek another means of escape. If not, exit the room, close the door behind you and leave the home quickly.

NOTE:

If SMOKE is present in the area, consider staying low and crawling below the level of the smoke.

⊚ **If you cannot leave a room,** place a wetted towel or other cloth at the bottom of the door, if possible, to limit the amount of smoke which could enter the room. A wetted cloth placed over the nose and mouth can also assist in preventing smoke from being inhaled, temporarily

⊚ **Once out of the home**, go to a neighbour and phone your local fire department immediately. **DO NOT RE-ENTER THE HOME** as you may be trapped or injured by the fire

 **If a severe thunderstorm occurs ....**

⊚ **Move vehicles into a garage** or other covered, sheltered area

---

- **Bring outdoor items, which could be damaged, into a covered sheltered area** or bring them indoors. If this is not possible, place them up against walls, as protection against hail damage

- **Shut down sensitive computer systems**, to protect them from power surges and potential power blackouts. Alternately, ensure adequate surge protection is available, based on the type of equipment used

- **If widespread power outages occur**, follow advice listed in the section, "If a power disruption occurs", above

- **Listen to news reports, to determine whether a tornado watch or warning is in effect** for your local area. Be aware of conditions outside your home, and take appropriate actions immediately, if a tornado is sighted. See advice under the section "If a tornado occurs"

- **Follow appropriate advice given in other sections as required**, related to disruptions to heating or water, power outages and other emergencies

 **If a flood warning is issued and your property could be affected......**

- **If water is rising too quickly to construct dykes**, if flash flooding is occurring, or if floodwaters are threatening to isolate your property, take your emergency supplies, evacuate all family members and move to a safe location **IMMEDIATELY**

- **If time is available, and you wish to enhance**

protection for your property, identify the most critical external areas which must be protected, based on the time available to you. Be realistic in your assessment, as significant time and effort will be required to construct flood control structures over a wide area

> *NOTE:*
>
> *Government agencies <u>may</u> be able to assist you in construction of flood control structures for your property. However, in a major flood occurring over a widespread area, they must prioritize use of limited government resources, to provide maximum protection to the greatest number of individuals.*

◉ **Ensure you have sufficient appropriate dyke building and flood protection materials** including sand, sandbags (burlap or plastic), shovels, plywood, plastic sheeting, etc. based on the area to be protected. Constructing dykes is physically demanding work. It should only be attempted by individuals who have no health related conditions and can perform the work safely

◉ **Get as much help as possible** for dyke construction

As a rule of thumb, it takes two fit, strong, people about one hour to fill and place 100 sandbags on a dyke, which will construct a dyke approximately 6 metres (20 feet) long by 30 centimetres (1 foot) high. Other guidelines for dyke construction are given below

---

General Guidelines for Dyke Construction (per 30 metres / 100 linear feet of dyke)		
Height of dyke		Approximate
Centimetres	Feet	Number of Bags required
30	1	500
60	2	2000
90	3	3,400

Source: Helping Yourself in an Emergency, Alberta Public Safety Service

⊚ **Identify the means within your home by which floodwaters can enter a building.** Typical outlets, which may allow water to seep into your home, include sewer traps, sinks, toilet bowls, bathtubs, laundry vents, and window wells in a basement area. Try to limit this means of seepage by plugging, if possible, but only if safe to do so

⊚ **Inspect sewer check valves,** if installed in your sewer trap, to see if they are working properly. If sufficient warning time exists, consider installing a check valve in sewer traps which do not have them

⊚ **Consider sending sick, elderly, or disabled adults, children, and pets to safe locations** away from areas of potential flooding, well in advance, if a flood is imminent

⊚ **Check non-perishable food stocks** to ensure they are sufficient, based on the number of people who will be remaining in the home (see the Supplies and Equipment section, under Home Emergency Preparedness, for suggested quantities and types of items). Move non-perishable food supplies, located in basement areas, to higher areas of the home for storage

⊚ **Check your home emergency kit,** and ensure

all required supplies are present (see the Supplies and Equipment section under Home Emergency Preparedness for suggested items, if a kit has not been prepared already). Move the kit to a higher level of the house, if it is normally stored in a basement area

⊚ **Store additional drinking water reserves** in clean containers, washbasins, and clean bathtubs in higher levels of the home. (See the Supplies and Equipment section under Home Emergency Preparedness for containers and other information if required)

⊚ **If time permits, remove all valuables from basements**, or other levels that could be flooded. Relocate them to the highest levels available in the house, if possible or practical

⊚ **Move electrical appliances and computers to the highest area available** and leave them in an unplugged state, to prevent potential safety concerns if water does rise and flood the area they are in. Water, being an excellent conductor, can transfer electricity, causing the potential for electrocution, if the flood has not cut off power

NOTE:

ONLY ATTEMPT TO SHUT OFF ELECTRICAL SOURCES IN A BASEMENT IF IT IS SAFE TO DO SO, as attempting to access a basement after it is flooded can result in electrocution.

⊚ **Back-up critical computer data**, if time is available, and transfer important documents to safe locations in

the house, away from the flood

- **Ensure your vehicle has a full tank of gas at all times**. In a flood, power may be cut off making gas pumps inoperable

- **Plan your evacuation route**, and determine what primary and secondary route(s) are available, if the roads are flooded

- **Listen to radio and television reports from local stations** for emergency information updates. If power fails, use a portable radio, from your emergency kit, to receive emergency updates

- **Move to a safe location IMMEDIATELY** if flooding cannot be safely controlled and threatens your personal safety

 TORNADOS

Tornadoes are violently rotating funnels of air, extending from a cloud to the ground. They typically occur during a severe thunderstorm, and occasionally during tropical storms or hurricanes. Multiple tornadoes can be created from a single storm.

Wind speeds in a tornado can exceed 400 kilometres per hour (250 miles per hour). Tornadoes, on average, travel 10-15 kilometres (7-9 miles), in a path 185 metres (200 yards) wide. Severe tornadoes have been reported which are 1.6 kilometres (1 mile) wide, traveling 70 kilometres (50 miles) before dissipating. Tornadoes can change direction without warning.

Tornadoes have been reported traveling at speeds exceeding 100 kilometres (60 miles) per hour, although most tornadoes move at much slower speeds.

Emergencies involving tornadoes can occur with little warning. The high winds associated with tornadoes, and suspended debris, can destroy homes, uproot trees, and move large heavy objects over great distances. Tornadoes tend to suck objects upwards, and hurl objects outwards in the area they affect.

If a tornado occurs ....

⊚ **Seek shelter inside if you are near your home when a tornado occurs**. Warn members of your family. Get your emergency kit and take it with you, if sufficient time is available

  - In **homes with storm cellars**, seek shelter in the storm cellar immediately

  - In **homes with basements,** take cover in the deepest and most sheltered area of the basement, away from windows if possible. Extra protection may be afforded by sheltering under heavy furniture, workbenches, or other well-constructed objects

NOTE:

Sheltering in small closets, small rooms or under stairways to the basement may also afford added protection.

- In **homes without basements,** seek shelter in a small, well-constructed room in the center of the home, if possible, or under heavy well-constructed furniture. Stay away from windows. Shelter on the ground level of the home, as higher levels are less safe in this type of emergency

- In **high-rise buildings**, use fire exit stairways to descend to lower levels, if time permits. Basement levels are the safest. If limited or no time is available, seek shelter in an interior hall, a closet or a small room with well-constructed walls, if possible, or under heavy, furniture. Stay away from windows

- If you are in a **mobile home, vehicle, or cannot reach your home,** seek shelter in a permanent building in the lowest level possible. If no permanent shelter is available, attempt to seek shelter in an open low-lying area, such as a ravine or ditch. Avoid forested areas, which may generate large amounts of flying debris

NOTE:

In an emergency involving a tornado, LOWER IS SAFER!

- **Use items from your emergency kit, if available, and as required**, and remain in place. Listen to radio reports, with a portable radio, to determine when a tornado warning has ended

- **If utilities or services are knocked out by the**

tornado, follow appropriate advice, given in other sections, related to water, heating, power outages, or any other emergencies

HURRICANES OR TYPHOONS

Hurricanes, known as typhoons in Asia and the Pacific regions, are large, powerful tropical storms, which form at sea. Hurricanes are cyclonic in nature, with winds and rain swirling around a central area of calm known as an "eye", which averages about 25 kilometres (15 miles) across. Hurricanes may cover a circular area of between 300 and 760 kilometres (200-500 miles) in diameter.

A hurricane is defined as a tropical storm with winds exceeding 118 kilometres per hour (74 miles per hour). Winds in a hurricane can reach 320 kilometres per hour (200 miles per hour). Hurricanes can be extremely destructive, due to the high winds, tidal surges and flash flooding. Thunderstorms and tornadoes can also occur, as a result of hurricane conditions.

Hurricanes are identified by satellite when they form, and are tracked on a continuous basis until the storm dissipates. Average warning time, for an area, which may be affected by a hurricane, is between three and four days.

If a hurricane is predicted for your area ....

⊚   **Follow news reports on a continuous basis,** to determine when the hurricane is expected to hit your area, as well as the expected magnitude and strength of the hurricane

- **If no specific evacuation order has been given for your area**, still consider evacuating the area and moving further inland or to a government recommended evacuation centre temporarily, based on your own assessment of conditions, or if recommended to do so by emergency officials

NOTE:

If a major storm is expected, and an evacuation order <u>has</u> been issued for your area, secure your home (see recommendations below), and evacuate the area as quickly as possible. Many fatalities have resulted in severe hurricanes, where people have ignored an evacuation order and stayed in place to attempt to protect their property from the storm.

To prevent as much damage as possible to your home during a hurricane:

- **Bring moveable outdoor items indoors**, if time permits, as lawn furniture, trash cans, children's toys, garden equipment, portable gazebos, or plant boxes and hanging plants could fly around and damage the surrounding area. Try to anchor objects which cannot be brought indoors

- **Do not cut off dead branches on trees or shrubs**, as loose limbs and debris which have not been hauled away can litter the ground, or fly around and damage the surrounding area

- **Remove loose items on fences and trees**, including unripened fruit, loose hanging ornaments and other items, which can break off and blow around. Store these items indoors until the storm is over

- **Consider removing antennas and/or satellite dishes**, which can be ripped off and blow around, if time permits. Store these items indoors until the storm is over

- **Move vehicles into a garage or sheltered area**, to protect from damage due to flying debris

- **If possible, cover the outside of windows with shutters**, designed to protect windows from flying debris, or place plywood covering over the windows and doors

- **Move electronic equipment such as televisions, stereos, computers, any other electronic equipment, and easily moveable appliances away from windows**, into the center of the home and to higher levels if time permits, wrap these items with blankets, bed sheets, and plastic sheeting to provide additional protection

- **Consider moving and storing extremely valuable or irreplaceable items** to safer locations, away from the hurricane impact area, or into anchored safes or other protective areas in the home

- **Consider photographing or videotaping property within your home**, as a record for insurance purposes

If you do plan to remain in your home throughout a hurricane:

- **Check your emergency kit**, and make sure all necessary supplies and equipment are present

- **Check stocks of non-perishable food** and get additional

supplies as necessary

- **Fill containers and temporary reservoirs in your home with water** (eg. bath tubs, sinks)

- **Fill your vehicle with gasoline**, in case you need to leave quickly

- **Obtain a supply of money sufficient for a few days** to a week of expenses

- **If you remain in your home and utilities or services are knocked out by the hurricane**, follow appropriate advice given in other sections related to water, heating, power outages and other emergencies, in previous chapters

 ## If a windstorm is forecast for your area ...

- **Bring moveable outdoor items indoors**, if time permits, as lawn furniture, trash cans, children's toys, garden equipment, portable gazebos, or plant boxes and hanging plants could fly around and damage the surrounding area

- **Do not cut off dead branches on trees or shrubs**, as loose limbs and debris can fly around and damage the surrounding area

- **Remove loose items on fences and trees**, loose hanging ornaments and other loose items, which can break off and blow around. Store these items indoors until the storm is over

- **Move vehicles into a garage** or sheltered area, to attempt to limit potential damage from flying debris

- If you remain in your home and utilities or services are knocked out by the wind storm, follow appropriate advice given in other sections related to water, heating, power outages and other emergencies

 ## If an earthquake occurs in your area ...

If you are indoors when the earthquake occurs:

- Get under a well constructed desk or table, or move into a hallway or against an inner wall in the building

- Avoid rooms like kitchens which may contain large numbers of stored objects that could fall on you

- Avoid windows, which could shatter, as well as areas with bookcases, large upright furniture or large appliances, which could topple and cause injuries

- Do not attempt to run downstairs while the quake is occurring, as you may lose your balance or trip and fall, causing serious injury

- Do not rush outside a large building while the quake is occurring, as you may be hit by falling glass and debris, causing serious injury

If you are outside when an earthquake occurs:

- Get into the open, away from buildings, power lines, chimneys or other free standing objects, which can topple and fall

- **Avoid tall buildings**, where falling glass and debris may be present

Once the initial quake is over:

- **Be aware that additional aftershocks may occur** at any time, and plan accordingly
- **Wear sturdy hard soled shoes to prevent injury from broken glass and debris** lying on the ground
- **If your emergency kit is accessible**, retrieve it and use stored supplies as required
- **Search for people who may be injured**, giving necessary first aid as required. Do not attempt to move seriously injured persons, unless they are in immediate danger of additional injury if no action is taken. Seek medical assistance as required but be aware that available paramedical services may be committed elsewhere
- **Put out small fires in your home using available fire fighting equipment**, if it can be done safely with available resources. Call for emergency assistance, but be aware that it may not be immediately available in an earthquake, as all available fire resources may be committed elsewhere
- **Do not use open ignition sources such as lighters or matches and electrical equipment or appliances**, including telephones, until you are sure there are no gas leaks in or around your home

NOTE:

If the smell of gas is present within your home or the surrounding area, evacuate the home and contact your local fire department <u>immediately.</u>

- **Shut off the main gas valve coming into your home**, if possible and safe to do so, if you suspect a gas leak may be present, but are not sure. Do not turn the gas back on until your local gas company has checked for leaks

- **Shut off electricity into the home**, if the earthquake has damaged electrical wiring

- **Stay away from downed power lines** and any objects that they are in contact with, to avoid the potential for serious injury or electrocution

- **Approach potentially damaged areas of your home with caution**, and avoid structures such as freestanding chimneys, or upright furniture such as bookcases, which could still collapse in an aftershock. Be aware that items present in cupboards or in enclosed shelving may have shifted and may tumble out when a door is opened

- **Clean up any small spills of potentially harmful household materials**, such as corrosive cleaning chemicals, solvents, pesticides, gasoline or other petroleum products, to eliminate potential safety concerns for yourself or your family. Use gloves, boots and other appropriate protective clothing while dealing with harsh chemicals. Seek assistance from emergency agencies immediately if a large spill has occurred in or near your home

- **If you remain in your home and utilities or services are knocked out by the earthquake**, follow appropriate advice given in other sections related to water, heating, power outages and other emergencies

 ## If a forest fire occurs ....

- **If the fire is large and is moving very quickly** or is threatening to isolate your property, take your emergency supplies, evacuate all family members, and move to a safe location **IMMEDIATELY**

In a widespread forest fire, conditions can change extremely quickly. If a wind shift occurs, and high winds are present, a fire front can travel many kilometres (miles) in the span of just one hour. Fires near inhabited areas can spread extremely quickly and engulf whole subdivisions. It is therefore important to monitor fire conditions on a continuous basis.

Fire agencies in and around your community will most likely be entirely committed to fighting a major forest fire. In situations of this nature, fire-fighting priorities are protection of LIFE as a primary responsibility - protection of homes and other property are considered of secondary importance if lives are being threatened.

- **If sufficient time is available and the forest fire is not immediately threatening your home:**

  - **Check your emergency supplies,** and have them readily accessible, if you must move quickly

  - **Gather all additional items together,** that you may require, if an evacuation is ordered

(use your evacuation checklist to assist in this task if one has been prepared in advance – see "Evacuation Checklist" under the Information section above)

- **Ensure your vehicle has a full tank of gas at all times**, if you are required to evacuate your home on short notice

- **Plan your evacuation**, and determine what the primary evacuation route would be from your home. Try to have a secondary route(s) available if the your primary route is cut off by the fire

- **Consider sending sick, elderly, or disabled adults, children, and pets to safe locations away from forest fire affected areas**, well in advance of a fire reaching your immediate area

- **Consider removing more valuable items from your home,** and storing them in safer locations, with a responsible relative or friend, until the forest fire emergency is over

- **Consider clearing brush and other flammable materials** at least 10 metres (30 feet) back from your home. Remove low hanging branches on trees, and tree branches that overhang your roof. Dispose of accumulated flammable debris in another location, or well away from the home

- **Keep areas like driveways clear**, to allow quick access by fire crews

- **Listen to radio and television reports from local stations** on a continuous basis for emergency information updates. If power fails, use portable radios to receive emergency updates

- In high fire hazard conditions, avoid smoking outside your home, and throwing smoldering cigarette ashes or butts on the ground. Tinder dry vegetation can ignite, and a fire can quickly spread over a wide area from just one small ignition source

- Move to a safe location as quickly as possible if a forest fire is advancing on your home and threatens your personal safety, or if ordered to do so by local officials

 ## If a blizzard or ice storm is forecast ....

- Follow news reports on a continuous basis, to determine when the blizzard or ice storm is expected to hit your area, as well as the expected magnitude and duration of the storm

- Check your emergency kit, and make sure all necessary supplies and equipment are present

- Check stocks of non-perishable food and get additional supplies as necessary

- Fill containers and temporary reservoirs in your home with water (eg. bath tubs, sinks)

- Fill your vehicle with gasoline, if needed for various emergency purposes

- Obtain a supply of money sufficient for a few days to a week of expenses, if the storm closes banks and ATM machines

- If you remain in your home, and utilities or services are knocked out by the blizzard, follow appropriate advice given in other sections related to water, heating, power outages and other emergencies

If extremely hot weather is occurring …

In hot weather, ambient temperatures may occur which are above the internal temperatures the human body requires to function normally and efficiently. Like any other object, which is heated, the internal temperature of the human body will attempt to rise to the ambient temperature of the surrounding area. High body temperatures can damage the brain and other vital internal organs, as well as disrupt vital chemical biological and electrical processes.

Self-regulating mechanisms, such as sweating, are present within the body to attempt to compensate for rapid internal temperature rises. However, in extreme temperature conditions, sweating may not be sufficient to control the body's internal temperature. In high humidity sweat may not evaporate quickly enough to dissipate heat. In addition, the age of an individual, obesity, poor circulation, drug or alcohol use, dehydration, or various diseases, can contribute to a number of heat related conditions, including heat stroke, heat exhaustion, and heat cramps.

General heat preparedness measures

⊚ **Drink fluids on a regular basis**, even if you are not thirsty. Plain, cool water is the best beverage for keeping fluids at proper levels in the body in extreme heat. Sport beverages (eg. GatorAde) can replace salts and minerals lost by sweating. If you have an existing medical condition which requires you to limit water intake, or are on a low salt diet, consult with your doctor as to what procedure should be followed, related to the consumption of water or sports beverages

NOTE:

AVOID drinking alcoholic beverages, beverages containing caffeine, or beverages with large amounts of sugar in extremely hot weather, as these beverages may cause you to lose fluids more rapidly.

AVOID extremely cold beverages, as the difference in temperature in extreme heat may cause stomach cramps.

◉ **Stay indoors**, if possible, in a cool place. Air conditioning or air circulating devices (eg. fans) can assist in maintaining comfortable temperatures in extremely hot weather. If air conditioning is not available in your home, consider spending the hottest part of the day in a public area which is air conditioned, such as a shopping mall, library or other temperature controlled building

◉ **Wear light, loose fitting clothing.** Clothing which is white or light coloured will help reflect heat. Avoid dark clothing, if possible, as it will absorb heat

◉ **Take a cool shower or bath**, to attempt to regulate body temperature

◉ **Rest regularly** and limit strenuous activity as much as possible

◉ **Check regularly for signs of heat exhaustion or heat stroke** especially in children, elderly individuals, people who have an illness such as heart disease or high blood pressure, or other persons who may be at risk and are living in your home

Symptoms could include but not be limited to:

Heat Exhaustion	Heat Stroke
Heavy sweating	Extremely high body temperature (above
Paleness	35 Celsius (103 degrees Fahrenheit,
Dizziness	measured orally)
Muscle cramps	Red, hot dry skin (no sweating)
Tiredness	Rapid, strong pulse
Weakness	Throbbing headache
Headache	Dizziness
Nausea or vomiting	Nausea
Cool moist skin	Confusion
Fast weak pulse	Unconsciousness
Fast shallow breathing	

For mild symptoms of heat exhaustion, items listed previously in this section can assist in making the person comfortable. Heat exhaustion may lead to heat stroke, if it is ignored.

NOTE:

For severe symptoms of heat exhaustion, or potential heat stroke, especially if the affected person suffers from a heart condition or high blood pressure, implement appropriate first aid measures and call for medical assistance immediately.

- **Check or visit with persons who are at risk** on a regular basis, if they are living in other locations affected by extreme heat conditions (rule of thumb – at least twice daily). Monitor them for signs of heat related illnesses

If outdoor activities must be undertaken:

- **Undertake activities in the morning or early evening,** as these are the coolest parts of the day

- **Drink fluids such as cool water regularly,** especially if exercising or working vigorously (rule of thumb – 2 to 4 glasses per hour). Sports beverages may be considered as part of fluid intake, to replenish salt and minerals

- **Rest on a frequent basis,** in a shady area

- **Cover your head, to keep cool,** to limit potential for heat exhaustion or heat stroke

- **Wear UV protective sunglasses and sunscreen** of at least SPF 30 on exposed skin, to prevent sunburn and other sun related skin conditions

- **Never leave a child or animal in a hot vehicle** for extended periods of time, even with windows opened partially. The temperature in a vehicle interior in hot weather can rise rapidly, causing heat stress and potential injury or death

 **If a chemical or petroleum release occurs near your home or near your community …**

Releases of chemical or petroleum related materials into the environment could have a significant impact on your home in an emergency.

Spills or releases of solids on the ground can dissolve in water. Liquid materials on ground normally affect only a localized area in the short term, but can penetrate soil and contaminate underground drinking water supplies on a long-term basis.

Spills of soluble solid materials or liquids, directly into a watercourse, can contaminate drinking water sources at the water intake for your community.

Releases of gaseous materials from pressurized storage vessels, whether at a fixed facility such as a propane tank at a gas station, an industrial plant, or from a tank mounted on a vehicle, or train, can significantly impact a wide area. Actual impact on the surrounding area could change rapidly and constantly, depending on changing meteorological conditions and varying wind directions, which could occur during the release. Chemical materials that are flammable can pose a potential fire or explosion hazard, if ignited.

Many point ignition sources exist in a major community, including electrical devices, power lines, and powered vehicles. Some flammable materials are also heavier than air, seeping into low-lying areas such as basements, where they may be ignited by a pilot light from a furnace. Flammable vapours can also enter a home through a dry sewer trap causing additional fire or explosion hazards.

Other hazardous materials may be toxic, poisonous, corrosive, radioactive or exhibit other properties which may affect humans, animals, property or the environment. In all cases quick action may need to be undertaken, to protect yourself or your family from the effects of the spill or release.

General precautions

- **Monitor radio or television reports** related to the emergency, to determine whether your home or family could be impacted by the chemical release

- **Follow any specific directives** given by government authorities related to the emergency. Officials, directing response to the emergency, are best able to determine what is required, to protect the safety of the individuals who may be affected by events which are occurring, either on a localized or wide spread basis

- **If you remain in your home** and utilities or services are unavailable due to the chemical release, follow appropriate advice given in other sections related to water, heating, power outages and other emergencies

NOTE:

Do not assume that a major emergency release of a gas into the atmosphere, even if it has occurred a number of kilometres or miles from your home, cannot impact you or your family. If meteorological conditions are right, and your home is potentially downwind of the release, you can be impacted.

As a rule of thumb, weather forecasters report wind direction giving the direction the wind is blowing from. The downwind direction is the location that the wind is blowing towards (eg. if the wind is reported as north, the wind is blowing downwind towards the south).

Also consider that wind conditions are variable, and may change constantly. While you may not be downwind of the release currently, you may be downwind if conditions change. As a major gas release may continue for several hours to days, if not controlled, weather forecasts may need to be monitored, on a regular basis, throughout the duration of the emergency.

Spills into watercourses can contaminate a community's water supply, even if the community is many kilometres or miles downstream from the original emergency site. Events may cause the water supply to be shut down abruptly and for an extended period to protect the safety of the community affected.

Plan accordingly, if you could be affected, based on your own assessment of the situation, and advice from emergency officials in your community.

Evacuation

In cases where hazardous materials may threaten lives in an emergency, localized or wide spread evacuation may be undertaken in the potential impact area.

If time and conditions permit, evacuations could be undertaken to limit exposure to toxic, poisonous or corrosive gas releases.

Depending on the conditions in a gas release of this nature, consideration may also be given to sheltering in-place for some or all residents in the potential impact area. (See In-Place Sheltering in the section below for further information).

In many jurisdictions, government authorities have the legal right to undertake forced evacuation of an area, if certain legal conditions have been met. You may be required to leave your home on extremely short notice, even if you do not perceive any immediate danger in your surrounding area.

If the chemical or flammable material release is posing an immediate hazard to your home:

⊚   **Evacuate all family members** and move to a safe location **IMMEDIATELY**

If sufficient time is available and the release is not immediately threatening your home:

⊚   **Check your emergency supplies**, and have them readily accessible, if you must move quickly

⊚   **Gather all additional items together** that you may require, if an evacuation is ordered (use your evacuation checklist to assist in this task if one has been prepared in advance – see "Evacuation Checklist" under the Information section above)

- **Ensure your vehicle has a full tank of gas** at all times, if you are required to evacuate your home on short notice

- **Plan an evacuation route**, if required, and determine what the primary evacuation route would be from your home, if an evacuation were ordered. Try to have a secondary route(s) available if the your primary route is unavailable

- **Consider sending sick, elderly, or disabled adults, children, and pets to safe locations** which cannot be affected by the release, well in advance of a potential impact

If an evacuation is ordered by government authorities in a chemical or flammable material release:

- **Follow specific instructions given by local emergency authorities**, including following any particular evacuation routes indicated in the instructions

In most cases, a particular evacuation route has been specified, for safety purposes, to prevent evacuees from entering the area where a flammable or toxic gas cloud may be present, or to prevent them from driving into other areas where there may be a safety issue. Avoid using your favourite shortcut out of the area, as it may place you in danger.

In-place sheltering

During major releases of toxic gaseous chemicals into the atmosphere, which could potentially affect a large populated area, government officials may recommend **In-Place Sheltering** as opposed to **Evacuation** during the emergency.

This may be done in situations where it is felt that the risks of exposure to a hazardous airborne chemical in the open air, during a major evacuation, outweighs the risks of having persons remain, in place, in their home.

The concept of in-place sheltering is not difficult to understand. Your home is normally a life support system for your family, providing shelter and comfort. Especially in climates where severe cold weather conditions are normal at certain times of the year, houses are well sealed and insulated against the elements. Even if all doorways and windows are tightly sealed in an insulated home, sufficient breathable air remains in most homes for many hours.

Decisions related to in-place sheltering are intended for emergency conditions which are hours in duration. Emergency conditions that may last days or weeks would require the evacuation of affected persons to other safe locations, on an extended basis.

Local emergency authorities are the best source of information related to what you should do, especially if they request you to shelter in-place. However, if limited information has been provided as to what to do, consider the following items:

⊚ **Take immediate action** to shelter in-place, if a government or other advisory to do so is issued, as time may be critical. Quickly bring all members of your family, pets or others indoors

⊚ **Close and seal** all windows and exterior doors, to prevent them from opening unexpectedly

⊚ **Turn off all fans, heating or air conditioning units**, or any other devices, which draw air into the home from the outside. Toxic vapours could be drawn into the house from external air exchange in an emergency

◉ **Close external vents** which connect directly to the outside, as well as fireplace dampers

◉ **Consider sealing around external doors** with duct tape and placing and taping plastic sheeting over windows, if these supplies are available and time permits. If limited time or supplies are available, concentrate your efforts on sealing around any doors, windows, or vents into, or near, the room you will be sheltering in

◉ **Get your personal emergency kit** and keep it with you at all times. Consider bringing a supply of food, water and other personal comforts for you and your family as well. Make sure your emergency portable radio or other communications devices you want to use are working properly, and are in the sheltered area with you

◉ **Go to an interior room in the home** without windows, if possible. Preferably the room should be above ground level, as some gaseous chemicals are heavier than air and will seep into basements or other low-lying areas. The room should be large enough for all persons to sit comfortably

◉ **Choose a location with a hard wired telephone, if possible,** (eg. a standard telephone that does not require additional AC power) for communications with your emergency contacts, or to report a life-threatening situation. Cellular phones may also assist in emergency communications. Limit use of communications devices, as telephone communications equipment may be overwhelmed with calls, severely limiting the ability for important calls to get through

◉ **If pets are in the home,** bring them into the room with you. Ensure you have your pet's emergency supplies with you, as well as a supply of food and water for them

- **Monitor reports** about the emergency on your radio, television or other communications device, until you are told it is safe to leave your shelter, or until you receive further instructions from local emergency authorities

PERSONAL PREPAREDNESS IN YOUR OFFICE

Every company should have an emergency plan that outlines response procedures for various emergency conditions, which may affect employees at their facilities. Many companies have extremely good emergency plans that are maintained and exercised on a regular basis including contingencies related to specific emergencies which could occur within the office environment, as well as scenarios for evacuation of the offices, or building, if required in an emergency.

Many of these emergency plans, especially in high-rise or multi-tenant buildings, are coordinated between multiple companies, and include building administrators as part of the planning process.

With this in mind, few individuals consider planning personally for an emergency which may occur in their office or work environment. However, in a major widespread emergency, where helping and protecting the greatest number of people becomes the priority, and where resources may be overwhelmed, individual considerations may become secondary.

You, personally, may also be indirectly affected by an emergency while at your office. A major snowstorm or other severe weather could strand you at the office for hours or a few days, after everyone else has left and services are closed. Would you be prepared to remain safe and comfortable with access to limited outside resources?

Preparedness at the office does not have to be as detailed or elaborate as preparedness in other locations, as many resources may be available within your company already. However, you may wish to consider obtaining a few items, for office emergency preparedness, as part of your personal emergency planning efforts.

Supplies and equipment

Consider having a **basic personal emergency kit** stored at your work location. Your basic emergency kit at work does not have to be as well equipped as the kit in your home, but should be sufficiently stocked to assist you in managing your own personal needs in an emergency.

Typical items stored in this type of basic kit could include:

- **A battery powered flashlight**, or a flashlight with an alternate power source that does not require batteries

- **A small battery powered portable radio**, or a radio with an alternate power source that does not require batteries

- **Fresh batteries** of appropriate type for each battery powered item

- **A warm blanket** (or "space blanket" type Mylar based substitute)

- **A multiplex pocketknife** (eg. "Swiss army" type knife) or multitool which performs similar functions

- **A small supply of high energy non-perishable foods** such as:
  - **Nuts** (unless allergic to these items)
  - **Dried fruit**
  - **Crackers,** cookies, or dry bread products
  - **Protein or fruit bars**
  - **Instant packaged soups,** chicken, beef, or vegetable

- **Bouillon cubes** or packets
- **Packaged instant meals** (eg. cup-'o'-noodles)

◉ **A small supply of bottled water**

◉ **A small supply of money** and/or change

More advanced items to consider include but are not limited to:

◉ **Feminine supplies** (if required)

◉ **A spare pair of prescription glasses**

◉ **A small supply of medications** you take normally

◉ **A personal size first aid kit** (most offices normally have first aid supplies stored in an easily accessible location but it is useful to be prepared personally)

◉ **A spare warm coat**, hat and gloves for unexpectedly cold weather

◉ **A pair of sturdy soled shoes**

◉ **Any equipment or supplies** related to other special needs you may have

Try to keep at least a day's worth supply of any necessary disposal items, and preferably two days or more if possible.

Items stored in your office emergency kit do not have to be new, or purchased specifically for that purpose. As example, older portable radios, which are not used frequently, but which still function correctly, may be stored in the kit. Older prescription glasses, which have been replaced with newer glasses, could also be stored in your emergency kit.

Try to keep all the items which form part of your emergency kit in the same location, preferably in a sturdy bag or box to ensure it is ready for use at all times. Make a list of the equipment and supplies, which should be present in the kit, and store it in the box with your supplies or on the outside of the box or bag.

If supplies are removed, or used in the emergency kit, replace them as soon as possible. Batteries, which are old or other supplies, which can expire, should be replaced as required.

Items in your emergency kit, like flashlights and radios, should be tested regularly (rule of thumb – at least every six months) to ensure they are functioning properly. Any batteries stored in these units should be checked at the same time, to ensure they are not leaking or corroding. If they have started corroding, they should be replaced as soon as possible with fresh batteries, to prevent equipment damage.

If you do not have an emergency kit in the office but have brought your vehicle to the office and cannot get home, consider getting your vehicle emergency kit and keeping it with you at all times until the emergency is over.

 **Emergency information**

As part of your personal emergency preparedness activities for the office, take a few minutes to determine what emergency supplies and equipment the company has provided and be aware of where these supplies are located. On the basis of what you find, you may wish to supplement these resources with additional supplies in your own basic emergency kit.

Review any posted emergency plans within your office, and

determine the location of the closest exits from the building to your office or work area. Also determine the location of the nearest alternate exits.

Finally, if you have any special needs, disabilities or other requirements, which could affect your safe evacuation from your workplace, discuss these needs with your immediate supervisor, building administrators and/or with other personnel in charge of emergency planning in your office or building. Ensure these needs have been taken into account as part of your company's work place emergency response plan. (See the "Emergency Planning for Special Needs section for further information).

TRAVEL PREPAREDNESS – ROAD VEHICLES

We, as a society, tend to use our vehicles frequently when traveling from place to place, and we rely on them to get us there safely. However, unexpected things can happen at any time, from severe weather events, to mechanical breakdowns, to accidents, all causing potential emergency conditions to occur.

In an emergency, we may have to rely on the resources present in the vehicle to sustain us and protect us until additional assistance arrives. If the vehicle is still functional and undamaged, it can also serve as a source of shelter and/or heat. It is therefore important to undertake a little emergency preparedness, as it relates to our automobiles.

 ## Supplies and equipment

Every motor vehicle you travel in regularly should have at least a basic emergency kit stored in it at all times.

Typical items stored in this type of basic kit include:

- ⊚ **Battery jumper cables**

- ⊚ **A small tool kit**, with common screwdrivers (straight, cross and square head), pliers (needle nose and regular), as well as any special tools specific for the vehicle you drive, or a multi-tool which performs similar functions

- ⊚ **A small shovel** and sack of sand

- ⊚ **Box of facial tissues** and/or moist towelettes

- ⊚ **A pocket knife and can opener**, or multi-tool which performs similar functions

- **Frost scraper and brush** (for cold weather climates)

- **A flashlight with spare batteries**, or a flashlight with an alternate power source

- **A blanket or blankets** if multiple persons regularly travel in a vehicle

- **A supply of non-perishable food** sufficient for one-two days for each person who regularly travels in the vehicle (tea, soup packets, non-perishable candy or granola bars, nuts, and other packaged items are good choices)

- **A bottle of water** per person usually traveling in the vehicle. Bottles of water can be omitted if cold weather conditions could cause the water to freeze and split the container open

- **Matches** and/or a disposable lighter

- **Candles**

- **A small first aid kit**, with sufficient supplies for one to two people (consider obtaining a larger kit, if more people regularly travel with you)

Where possible, store the emergency equipment for the vehicle in a sturdy bag, to ensure it remains together at all times. Make a list of the equipment and supplies, which are included in the kit, and store it, either inside, or attached to the outside of the bag. Consider marking the container "Emergency Kit" or "Emergency Use" with a permanent marker or other marking device.

If supplies are removed or used in the emergency kit, replace them as soon as possible. Non-perishable food items and old batteries should be replaced as required.

If an item is removed for other uses around the home, ensure that it is replaced in the vehicle as soon as possible. Damaged or non-functional items should be repaired or replaced as soon as possible.

Check your basic emergency kit regularly (rule of thumb, at least twice per year), and especially if you are going on a long trip or may encounter severe weather during a regular trip. Your life may depend on this equipment being available in the event of an emergency.

Every car or truck should also have a working car jack, and a functional spare tire stored in case of emergencies. Even if these items have never been used, they should be checked occasionally, to ensure they would be in working order when needed.

More advanced emergency preparedness equipment you may wish to carry with you includes:

◉ **A portable radio** with spare batteries, or one with an with alternate power source that does not require batteries. This may be especially important if your vehicle can only receive satellite radio signals, if you require local emergency information on AM/FM channels

◉ **A DC charging cord** for your cellular phone, to charge from the car battery

◉ **A small mechanical air compressor**, which runs off a car battery as a temporary solution to fix a flat tire

◉ **A power inverter**, which allows AC powered devices to be run off your vehicle battery

◉ **A portable searchlight**, which runs off a car battery

- **Hazard triangles**, road hazard flares, and/or portable battery powered lights for indicating that a stalled vehicle is up ahead

- **Chemical light sticks** (for emergency lighting)

- **A security key** compatible with any security lugs which hold your vehicle tires in place (if security lugs are installed on your vehicle)

- **A portable fire extinguisher**, suitable for putting out a fire in a vehicle

- **A small supply of money** and/or change for emergency purposes

If you can think of any other items that you would like to have available in an emergency, by all means include them in your emergency kit as well. The items listed above are just there to provide some guidance. Think about your personal situation and plan accordingly.

EMERGENCY PREPAREDNESS IS A MINDSET, NOT A RIGID SET OF RULES!

 ## Emergency information

As part of your emergency preparedness activities for road travel, familiarize yourself with your vehicle and its capabilities.

Owner's manuals contain various pieces of useful information on the operation of your vehicle. Familiarize yourself with the safety and emergency features of your vehicle when you purchase it. Note the locations and operation of various items, including but not limited to:

- **Storage locations for the spare tire and jack**. If these items are stored in closed compartments within the vehicle, determine how the compartment is opened if equipment is needed

- **Tow points on the vehicle.** Every vehicle is designed with tow points that allow a disabled vehicle to be towed or moved without damage. Determine where these points are located on your specific vehicle, if your vehicle becomes stuck and requires a tow

- **Hazard lights** are used to signal to others that your vehicle is disabled, and to mark the location of your vehicle, especially at night, to prevent collisions with other vehicles

Store your owner's manual with your vehicle at all times, for additional reference in an emergency. If the manual is unclear as to the location and function of any safety feature, consult with your vehicle dealership or the manufacturer for additional information.

 ## Regular travel

To prepare for regular day-to-day travel, you may wish to consider the following:

- **Check fuel levels** prior to travel to ensure you do not run out unexpectedly – try to keep your tank no less than half full at all times

- **Check fluid levels** and tire pressure on a regular basis (rule of thumb - monthly), and undertake preventative maintenance as required by your vehicle service guide, to limit the possibility of an unexpected breakdown

◉ **Check local weather conditions** for the day, and plan accordingly

If severe weather is occurring or expected later in the day, ensure your emergency kit is present in your vehicle, and carry additional supplies appropriate for conditions, as required (eg. extra warm clothing in cold weather).

◉ **If you have a cellular phone**, carry it with you in the vehicle, for emergency purposes. Try to keep it charged, for possible use in an emergency when traveling. Have a cellular phone charger cord for your specific phone available in your vehicle emergency kit, to allow the phone to be plugged into the DC utility outlet in your vehicle, to charge from the car battery, if required

◉ **If possible also carry a telephone directory** or emergency number listings for your local area

As an additional item of emergency preparedness, you may wish to become a member of an automobile association affiliated with the Canadian Automobile Association (CAA) or the American Automobile Association (AAA), as these associations can provide roadside emergency or towing assistance, as part of the services provided with membership.

Travel on long trips

If you are planning a long trip in an automobile, you may want to consider the following preparations:

- ◉ **Have your vehicle checked** physically and mechanically prior to the trip

  - **A working vehicle** goes a long way towards ensuring that you will not be stranded unexpectedly

- ◉ **Obtain maps of the area** through which you will be traveling

  - **Maps for many areas of North America, Europe, Australia, New Zealand and many other foreign countries** are readily available for free to members by contacting affiliates of the Canadian Automobile Association (CAA) or American Automobile Association (AAA). Some maps may also be available at service stations or your local bookstores

- ◉ **Check that all your basic emergency equipment and supplies are present** and functional

  - **If the number of people traveling in the vehicle is more than is regularly present**, consider carrying extra basic personal supplies like blankets, and non-perishable food

  - **Carry a supply of water with you**, sufficient for at least a day for every person, and refill or purchase extra water as it is used while traveling

- ◉ **Check weather reports** for conditions in the areas you will be traveling

  - **Plan for conditions**, and carry any additional supplies (eg. extra warm winter clothing, socks, rain suits or coats) which may be required, based on forecast conditions

- **Determine if any travel advisories are in effect for the areas where you will be traveling.** Provincial and state agencies are available in various areas, which provide this information via a local telephone number or on the Internet

- **If severe weather is expected** where you plan to travel on a particular day, (eg. snow or ice storms, thunderstorms, hurricanes), consider delaying travel until the severe weather subsides

- **Make sure you have adequate fuel** for the vehicle throughout the trip

  - **Have a full fuel tank at the start.** Always keep a reserve supply of fuel in your tank (good rule of thumb – no less than a ½ a tank for long trips in remote areas), and look for a gas station once the reserve level in your tank is reached

  - **Ensure the vehicle has a full tank at the start of long distance travel** to areas where fuelling stations may be infrequent

- **If traveling to a remote location**, make sure someone is aware of when you are leaving, and when you plan to reach your destination, in case you become stuck or experience severe weather or mechanical difficulties

- **If you have a cellular phone**, carry it with you in the vehicle, and ensure that the battery remains charged, where possible. Consider renting a cellular phone, or borrowing one from a friend prior to undertaking the trip

- **DC adapter cables** (12 Volt) are available for many cellular phones, to allow the phone to be connected to the cigarette lighter or utility outlet of the vehicle – this is a quick way to recharge your cell phone battery

> *NOTE:*
>
> *Cellular coverage may not be present in all the specific areas you may travel in on a long trip, as many "dead zones" exist. However, availability of a cellular phone while traveling can assist greatly in emergency situations where coverage does exist.*

- **If you or your family require life sustaining medication** or other special supplies, ensure you carry a supply sufficient for your trip, plus a reserve of seven days extra, if possible

- **If a pet is traveling with you**, ensure that you have a supply of food and other necessities for your pet as well

- **Consider obtaining travel health insurance** for every person with you, when traveling to another country

  - **This insurance may be obtained from a variety of sources** including travel agencies and motor vehicle associations such as affiliates of the Canadian Automobile Association (CAA) or American Automobile Association (AAA). Insurance of this nature is relatively inexpensive, and may be taken out on a per trip basis or on a yearly basis for multiple trips per year

- **Carry a sufficient supply of money or travelers checks** with you for at least several days basic expenses

- **If an emergency occurs and you are stranded**, a bank or banking machines may not be easily accessible

In an actual emergency

If you come upon an accident where police and other emergency services have not arrived on the scene.

- **Determine if any injuries have occurred** to the people involved. Administer appropriate first aid measures, if required, and use emergency supplies in your vehicle to provide aid and comfort, as needed. Keep injured persons warm until help arrives

> *NOTE:*
>
> Do **NOT** move a person severely injured in an accident, unless it is absolutely necessary to save their lives or prevent further injury. Movement may result in additional injury or complications.

- **Telephone police to request assistance**, or request that other persons present at the site do this, using either a cellular phone or by traveling to the nearest telephone. Request medical services or fire services as well, if required

- **If you are tending to injuries**, and additional persons are present at the site, ask them to help direct traffic around the accident scene or assist you in other ways as necessary

- **Leave all items or debris present at the accident site where they are**, to assist authorities in their investigation of the accident scene

- **When emergency agencies arrive at the site**, assist them as required, and provide any information which they may request

 If caught in severe weather ...

- **Keep calm** and as relaxed as possible

- **Stay in the vehicle**, protected from the effects of the weather

- **If the engine is still operational in cold weather**, run it occasionally to heat the passenger compartment. Fuel will be conserved for a longer period of time using this method

NOTE:

If running the engine, check the exhaust pipe occasionally to ensure it remains clear of snow and debris at all times. A blocked exhaust pipe can cause exhaust fumes to enter the vehicle, with potential for asphyxiation or carbon monoxide poisoning.

- **Get the vehicle emergency kit** and have it with you at all times. Use supplies from it as required. Try to conserve food and water as much as possible, but ensure you eat regularly, especially in cold weather, as your body needs fuel to stay warm

- **Lower a window slightly** on the side of the vehicle away from the wind for ventilation purposes

- **Try to stay comfortably warm and dry.** Open clothing at the front, neck or wrists or remove outer layers as required to avoid overheating. Perspiration can cause discomfort, and reduce the insulative properties of damp clothing, resulting in a dangerous loss of body heat

- **Move occasionally** to stimulate circulation and keep extremities warm in cold weather

- **If you have a cellular phone** attempt to contact local emergency or police agencies to inform them of your location and situation, as required

- **Turn emergency flashers ON** when vehicles are approaching to try to signal for help. Turn them off to conserve remaining energy when no traffic is near by

- **Seek help in daylight** once the severe weather is over, and as hazardous conditions subside

NOTE:

In storms which cause poor visibility do not attempt to walk to find help as you may soon get disoriented and lost.

Do not leave your vehicle in dangerously cold weather with high wind chills, as you may soon freeze or suffer from frostbite or hypothermia.

 ## If a tornado is spotted while traveling...

- **If you spot a tornado occurring in the distance** on an open highway, **drive away from it and at right angles to its path**, if road options permit, and limited traffic is present. Most tornadoes travel at speeds that are below normal driving speeds on a highway. However, constantly monitor the direction that the tornado is traveling in, as tornadoes can frequently change direction and speed

- **If road conditions or options do not allow you to avoid the tornado**, leave your vehicle. Take your vehicle emergency kit with you if time permits. Vehicles can easily be picked up, tumbled and crushed by the force of the winds and debris, with the possibility of severe injury or fatality for anyone inside

- **Seek the best shelter you can find**, as most injuries from a tornado are from flying debris. **IN AN EMERGENCY INVOLVING A TORNADO, LOWER IS SAFER.** A basement or lower floor in a well-constructed permanent building or a storm cellar is best. Tents, mobile trailers, trailer homes, flimsy sheet metal outbuildings offer almost no protection, and may be picked up, crushed, or turned into missiles by tornado force winds and flying debris

- **If no permanent buildings are nearby**, seek natural shelter points, based on surrounding terrain. A cave or other similar sheltered location, especially in a low-lying area, may provide shelter from flying debris. Avoid forested areas, as trees may be uprooted, and additional flying debris may be created

- **If no other possible cover is available**, seek shelter in a low ravine or ditch and cover your head as much as possible to protect it from flying debris. Try to find something to hang on to if you are not completely sheltered, to avoid being carried away by the winds

 **If flash flooding occurs while traveling ...**

Flash flooding may occur as a result of a heavy rainstorm or thunderstorm. In a few minutes or even seconds, water can rise rapidly, and a dry streambed or a slow flowing watercourse may become a raging torrent.

In urban areas like underpasses, or low-lying areas along a roadway, water may quickly block the road making passage difficult or impossible. A vehicle may be carried downstream, or sink below the surface, if there is sufficient water, with the potential for injury or drowning fatality.

- **Avoid driving into water if you do not know the depth**. Water in a flash flood, blocking a road or in an underpass, may look shallow, but could be quite deep. Your vehicle could stall, stranding you in the middle of a torrent, or a deep pool of water, preventing you from escaping to safety

NOTE:

If heavy rains are occurring and you have reason to believe a flash flood may occur, stay out of low water crossings and streams. Water can rise rapidly and without warning.

- **Don't assume you can safely cross moving water.** In a flash flood, tremendous hydrodynamic pressure can be exerted, sufficient to overturn a vehicle, or knock a person off their feet. In addition, only 45 to 60 centimetres (18 to 24 inches) of water may be required to float a vehicle. Once a road vehicle is floating, the driver has no control, and may be swept away with the current

- **Debris** such as trees, gravel, rocks, and freestanding structures such as tanks, buildings and equipment may also be carried downstream with the current. Debris present in a torrent may knock a vehicle into the water, causing it to be swept away

- **Avoid driving in narrow canyons in a heavy rainstorm.** Narrow canyons may channel heavy rains, creating a flash flood, that can sweep a vehicle away

- **Exercise caution when driving in heavy rains in the mountains.** A flash flood can sweep across a road or trigger a mudslide or avalanche without warning, in a localized area. Flash flooding can also wash out a road quickly, or undermine a section of road, causing it to collapse under the weight of a vehicle

 ## If an earthquake occurs while traveling…

- **Stop carefully if on safe level ground.** Move your car out of traffic if possible

- **Do not stop under an overpass, or on a bridge**, as these structures may collapse

- **Avoid stopping in areas with overhead power lines**, overhead signs, light posts, or large trees, if possible, as these may fall or collapse on a vehicle unexpectedly

- **Avoid stopping by large buildings** if possible, as falling glass and debris, can cause severe injuries

- **Stay in your vehicle until the shaking stops**, as additional protection against falling debris

- **If you resume driving**, watch for breaks or sags in the pavement, fallen rocks, and bumps or buckling in the road. Avoid bridges, underpasses, or other free standing structures, if at all possible, as they may have been damaged and still could collapse as a result of the quake

 **If your vehicle is stuck or has mechanical problems...**

⊙ **Stay as calm as possible**

⊙ **Think about what can reasonably be done** and plan your actions accordingly, based on the resources you have available

⊙ **Examine your vehicle if a mechanical problem is suspected.** See if you can determine the problem, and if it is easily correctable. Refer to the owner's manual in your vehicle for reference as required

⊙ **If you try to get your vehicle unstuck**, work safely and slowly to prevent overexertion. Attempting to push a car, shovel heavy loads of mud or snow, or move other heavy objects can cause injury or heart attack. If an additional vehicle and equipment is available to help extricate your vehicle, ensure proper tow points on the vehicle are used to prevent damage

⊙ **Be aware that strong winds**, extremely cold temperatures, and driving rain or snow can increase any work hazards

⊙ **Attempt to stay as warm and dry as possible.** Rain, snow and perspiration can cause dampness, reducing the insulative properties of clothing. This can result in a dangerous loss of body heat

⊙ **If nothing can be done personally to free the stuck vehicle**, activate emergency flashers, raise the hood of the vehicle and attempt to flag down passing vehicles to obtain additional assistance

⊙ **Seek help in daylight at local dwellings.** In the

evening, evaluate whether you can safely seek help by leaving your vehicle, given the weather and local conditions. If you cannot or are unsure, remain with the vehicle until daylight, or until assistance arrives

⊚ **In severe weather**, stay with the vehicle, and follow the advice under "Severe Weather" listed above

 If stranded in a remote area ....

⊚ **Keep calm** and as relaxed as possible

⊚ **In darkness or severe weather**, stay in the vehicle, protected from the effects of the weather, and safe from wild animals

⊚ **If the engine is still operational in cold weather**, run it occasionally to heat the passenger compartment. Fuel will also be conserved for a longer period of time using this method

NOTE:

If running the engine, check the exhaust pipe occasionally to ensure it remains clear of snow and debris at all times. A blocked exhaust pipe can cause exhaust fumes to enter the vehicle, with potential for asphyxiation.

⊚ **Get the vehicle emergency kit and have it with you at all times**. Use supplies from it as required. Try to conserve food and water as much as possible, but ensure you eat regularly in cold weather, as your body needs fuel to stay warm

- **Lower a window slightly** on the side of the vehicle away from the wind for ventilation purposes

- **Try to stay comfortably warm and dry**. Open clothing at the front, neck or wrists or remove outer layers as required to avoid overheating. Perspiration can cause discomfort, and reduce the insulative properties of damp clothing, resulting in a dangerous loss of body heat

- **Move occasionally to stimulate circulation** and keep extremities warm in cold conditions

- **If you have a cellular phone or radio** attempt to contact local emergency or police agencies to inform them of your situation

- **Turn emergency flashers on** when vehicles are approaching, in an attempt to signal for help. Turn flashers off to conserve remaining energy when no traffic is near by

- **Seek help in daylight once the severe weather is over**, and as hazardous conditions subside

NOTE:

In storms which cause poor visibility, do not attempt to walk to find help as you may soon get disoriented and lost. Do not leave your vehicle in dangerously cold weather with high wind chills, as you may soon freeze or suffer frostbite.

If you are lost...

◉ **Stop the vehicle and remain calm**

◉ **Use any reference maps** you have to determine where you may be

◉ **Attempt to double back** and follow the same route to your original starting point

◉ **Flag down any passing vehicles**, and ask directions from a passersby if available

◉ **If you have a cellular phone**, attempt to contact local authorities, and inform them of your situation. Try to provide them as much general information as possible related to your current location

◉ **If your vehicle is equipped with an option or you subscribe to a service to assist lost or stranded motorists**, contact this service to receive assistance

◉ **If your vehicle becomes stuck while lost**, follow the advice under "If your vehicle is stuck or has mechanical problems" listed above

◉ **In limited visibility or severe weather**, stop where you are and follow the advice under "Severe Weather" listed above

TRAVEL PREPAREDNESS - BOATS

Recreational boating is a common pastime in many countries, for either fishing, or pure pleasure. Travel in a boat can occur on freshwater rivers or lakes as well as on the ocean. In an emergency, boats may be stranded in remote locations or could flounder or sink due to mechanical difficulties, severe weather or a variety of accidents.

 ## Supplies and equipment

Every boat used for personal purposes should have emergency equipment and supplies stored on board at all times.

Government regulations on water and boating safety in North America outline minimum requirements for safety and emergency equipment, with the specific quantities which must be stored in personal watercraft used for recreational purposes (sometimes referred to as pleasure craft or watercraft). Usually, requirements are based on the size and type of craft, whether the craft is to be used on inland lakes and watercourses or on the ocean, as well as whether a motor is powering the craft, or not.

Typical types of equipment and supplies stored in watercraft for emergency purposes could include:

⊚ **Life jackets** or other personal floatation devices (eg. life buoys or rings)

⊚ **Heaving and towing lines**

⊚ **Oars or paddles**

- **Anchor and cable**, rope or chain

- **Watertight flashlight(s)**

- **A compass or other appropriate navigation devices**

- **Emergency signaling devices** (eg. type A, B or C flares and flare launching devices, as required)

- **Sound signaling devices** (whistles, bells or air horns)

- **Bailers, buckets or manual water pumps**

- **Fire extinguishers**

- **Navigation lighting** (for nighttime or low light use)

- **Axe**

- **Re-boarding devices** such as ladders (if the watercraft is of sufficient freeboard)

- **A working VHF marine radio** or other communication device (dependent on the type and size of vessel)

Information on minimum emergency equipment and supplies required for your specific type of craft may be obtained by contacting the agency in charge of boating safety in your country, as well as boating dealerships and manufacturers. Where required, all emergency equipment purchased for use in your watercraft should meet recognized certifications and standards identified by the appropriate government.

Useful telephone numbers and web sites

CANADA

Fisheries and Oceans Canada
Canadian Coast Guard – Office of Boating Safety
Safety Equipment Requirements

Web site
http://www.ccg-gcc.gc.ca/obs-bsn/equipment_e.htm
(English)
http://www.ccg-gcc.gc.ca/obs-bsn/equipment_f.htm
(French)
Office of Boating Safety Info line:
1-800-267-6687   E-mail: obs-bsn@dfo-mpo.gc.ca.

UNITED STATES

U.S. Coast Guard (USCG)
Safety Equipment Requirements
Web site
http://www.uscgboating.org/safety/fed_reqs/equ_refchart.htm
USCG Boating Safety Info line:
1-800-368-5647   E-mail: uscginfoline@gcrm.com

Additional emergency equipment and supplies you may wish to carry in your craft for emergency situations when traveling could include:

- ⊚ **A tool kit** and appropriate spare parts

- ⊚ **Your boat owners manual** or guide book, in a watertight bag or cover

- ⊚ **A portable marine weather radio**, and spare batteries, or a marine weather radio that operates on an alternative power source, in a water tight case (if a VHF marine radio is not installed in your boat)

- ⊚ **Spare flashlight batteries**

- ⊚ **Additional reserve fuel supplies**, as required, in appropriate approved storage containers

- **An emergency supply of drinking water** (rule of thumb 4.5 L per – one gallon per person) sufficient for at least a day for every person who will be aboard. Consider taking additional emergency water supplies for longer trips

- **High-energy, non-perishable food** in watertight containers, sufficient for at least a day, for every person who will be aboard. Consider taking additional emergency food supplies for longer trips

- **Appropriate spare clothing** in a watertight bag, based on potential weather conditions, which may be encountered (eg. rain, cold weather, etc.)

- **Appropriate navigational charts** and/or maps for the area you are traveling in

- **A first aid kit** of appropriate size based on the number of persons who may be traveling

  Typical items in a basic first aid kit for boat travel could include:
  - **Adhesive sterile fabric bandages** of various sizes (preferably ones that will stick even when wet)
  - **4-6 sterile gauze pads** (2 inch, 4 inch)
  - **2-3 triangular sterile triangular cloth bandages**
  - **2-3 rolls sterile roll bandages** (2 inch, 3 inch)
  - **Fabric adhesive tape** (preferably a brand that will stick even when wet)
  - **Pre-moistened antiseptic towelettes**
  - **Scissors**
  - **Tweezers**

- Rubbing alcohol
- Soap
- **An approved first aid manual** or handbook
- **Fasteners** such as safety pins
- **Pain relieving and anti-inflammatory medications** such as Aspirin, Tylenol, Advil, etc.

Additional items you may wish to include in your first aid kit could include:

- **Antibiotic ointment**
- **Tube of petroleum jelly or other lubricant**
- **Cotton swabs (eg. Q-Tips)**
- **Thermometer**
- **Medicine dropper**
- **Needle and thread**
- **Latex gloves**
- **Antacid tablets or liquids** (for upset stomach)
- **Anti-diarrhea medication**
- **Anti-nausea/motion sickness medication** (eg. Gravol)
- **Other seasickness medications**, as appropriate
- **Allergy medications**
- **Laxative medication**
- **Insect repellants** / insect bite treatment
- **Sunscreen** (at least SPF 30)

Where possible, store the emergency equipment for your boat in a sturdy watertight container to ensure it remains together at all times. Make a list of the equipment and supplies, which should be present, and store it in the container as well. Consider marking the container "Emergency Kit" or "Emergency Use" with a permanent marker or other marking device.

If supplies are removed or used in the emergency kit, replace them as soon as possible. Non-perishable food items and other stored supplies should be replaced as required. Damaged or non-functional items should be repaired or replaced as soon as possible.

Check your boat emergency equipment and supplies regularly, and especially before every trip. Consider carrying additional emergency equipment and supplies based on the number of persons on-board, the length of the trip and potential weather conditions. Your life may depend on this equipment being available in an emergency!

Training and information

In addition to ensuring that the proper emergency supplies and equipment are stored in your vessel, based on government requirements, you should consider being trained in appropriate safe boating procedures, to allow you to make informed decisions in an emergency.

 **Boating safety**

In Canada, the **Competency of Operators of Pleasure Craft Regulation** requires operators of pleasure craft, fitted with a motor and used for recreational purposes, to have documentation of proof of competency available at all times, in the form of a card or equivalent documentation. These regulations are currently being phased in, in stages, and all appropriate operators will be required to comply with the regulations by 2009.

To obtain proof of competency in Canada, an operator must successfully complete an accredited course and written test, recognized by the Canadian Coast Guard, which covers the following subjects:

- **Minimum safety equipment requirements** required on board your boat

- **The Canadian buoy system**

- **How to share waterways**

- **A review of all pertinent regulations**

- **How to respond in an emergency situation**

Information on specific requirements in Canada, as well as a listing of accredited course providers, is available from the Canadian Coast Guard.

Useful telephone numbers and web sites

Canadian Coast Guard – Office of Boating Safety
Competency of Operators Course Information
Web site
http://www.ccg-gcc.gc.ca/obs-bsn/equipment_e.htm
(English)
http://www.ccg-gcc.gc.ca/obs-bsn/equipment_f.htm
(French)
Office of Boating Safety Info line:
1-800-267-6687   E-mail: obs-bsn@dfo-mpo.gc.ca.

In the United States, beginner to advanced boating safety courses are offered by a variety of organizations, to meet various state and federal requirements related to boating safety:

U.S. Coast Guard (USCG)
Boating Safety Course Links
Web site
http://www.uscgboating.org/safety/safety_courses.htm

USCG Boating Safety Info line:
1-800-368-5647   E-mail: uscginfoline@gcrm.com

 Radio communication

⊙ **Take a course in proper radio communication procedures,** to ensure you understand proper radio communication protocol, and proper emergency procedures if you are communicating a distress signal via radio. Depending on your location and the type of radio equipment installed in your vessel, you may be required to have a valid radio operator's license to use this type of equipment

 First aid

⊙ **Take a course in basic first aid or cardiopulmonary resuscitation (CPR),** to teach you what can be done in a medical emergency, an accident or another emergency where injuries are involved. Consider taking a more

advanced first aid course, if available in your area, which focuses on marine related medical emergencies

Courses are available from the Red Cross, St. John's Ambulance and from other recognized organizations throughout North America and other countries (consult your local telephone directory for organizations in your area).

In addition, consider obtaining a first aid manual or handbook from a recognized first aid organization, and store copies in the first aid kit on your vessel.

For your trip

 **Prior to regular travel via boat...**

To prepare for regular travel via boat, you may wish to consider the following:

- ⊚ **Inspect your boat** for any visible sign of problems. Have these problems corrected prior to traveling

- ⊚ **Top up fuel levels prior to travel** to ensure you do not run out unexpectedly. Carry a reserve supply, as required, in appropriate approved storage containers

- ⊚ **Ensure your emergency equipment and supplies are present,** and readily accessible when required

- ⊚ **Ensure sufficient personal floatation devices are present**, based on the number of people who will be traveling

- ⊚ **Ensure all supplies, equipment and containers are**

stowed or secured neatly and properly, so they will not shift or blow overboard

- ◉ **Ensure boat batteries are properly stowed** in a battery box, and that terminals are properly covered, to prevent a fire or electrical short

- ◉ **Check local marine weather conditions** for the day, and plan accordingly. Consider delaying unnecessary travel if severe weather is expected before your trip is completed

- ◉ **Carry additional supplies appropriate for conditions**, if weather conditions are expected to change (eg. extra warm clothing in cold weather)

- ◉ **If you are required to have communications equipment** on your vessel, test the equipment prior to leaving, to ensure it is working properly

- ◉ **Know the carrying capacity of the boat**, and ensure it is not overloaded with passengers, equipment or supplies

- ◉ **Brief guests** who are unfamiliar with proper boating safety procedures, prior to leaving the dock, and determine if they are adequately equipped for the trip

- ◉ **Ensure all life jackets are being worn** in an appropriate manner

Prior to travel on long trips via boat ...

If you are planning a long trip in a boat, you may want to consider a couple of additional items of emergency preparedness, including:

- ⊚ **Have your vessel and associated equipment checked** physically and mechanically prior to the trip
  - • **Working equipment and a watertight vessel** goes a long way towards ensuring that an emergency related to the condition of the vessel does not occur
- ⊚ **Obtain navigational charts and/or maps** of the local area through which you will be traveling
- ⊚ **Check that all your required emergency equipment and supplies** are present and functional

If the number of people traveling in the vehicle is more than is regularly present, ensure that sufficient personal floatation devices are present for everyone, and consider carrying extra basic personal supplies like spare clothing, blankets, and non-perishable emergency food supplies.

- ⊚ **Carry a supply of water with you,** sufficient for at least one day for every person aboard, and refill or purchase extra water as it is used while traveling
- ⊚ **Check communications devices** to ensure they are working properly
  - • **Check your marine radio**, if you have one installed in the vessel
  - • **Explain proper radio usage to other persons traveling with you**, as well as appropriate radio communication procedures to follow in an emergency. Consider posting important emergency contact procedures beside the radio, for quick reference purposes
  - • **If you have a cellular phone**, carry it with you in the vessel, and ensure that the battery remains charged, where possible

- **Post appropriate marine emergency contact procedures** for a cell phone in an easily accessible location in the vessel

- **Carry a DC adapter cable** (12 Volt) if available for your cellular phone, to allow the phone to be connected to the cigarette lighter or utility outlet on the vessel

NOTE:

Cellular coverage may not be present in all the specific areas you may travel on your trip, as many "dead zones" exist. Cellular phones are not a good substitute for a marine VHF radio, as a cellular phone is a point-to-point source of communication, and has limited range without a repeater antenna present. A distress call on a marine radio can be heard over a wide area by multiple stations in an emergency.

However, if no other communication source is available, a cellular phone may assist greatly in emergency situations, where coverage does exist.

- ◉ **Check marine weather reports** for conditions in the areas you will be traveling

  - **Plan for conditions**, and carry any additional supplies (eg. extra warm clothing, socks, rain suits, etc.) which may be required, based on these conditions

  - **If severe whether is expected** where you plan to travel (eg. windstorms, rain squalls, thunderstorms, hurricane watch), consider delaying travel until the severe weather subsides

- **Ensure the vessel is fuelled adequately** throughout the trip
  - **Have a full fuel tank** at the start of the trip
  - **Always keep a reserve supply of fuel in your tank** or in storage in appropriate, approved containers (good rule of thumb – consider locating a refueling point when no less than a ½ the main tank full of fuel remains, especially if no reserve supply is carried). Plan refueling points in advance, and refuel as promptly as possible, once the reserve level in your tank is reached
  - **Top up fuel tanks at each destination**, if a refueling station is present
  - **Ensure the vessel has a full fuel tank** when traveling through isolated areas where fuelling stations may not be present

- **Provide a float plan** to a responsible individual or appropriate government agency, if traveling to a remote location or a long distance, and make sure that they are aware of when you are leaving, and when you plan to reach your destination. For individuals who are given a float plan and are unfamiliar with marine emergencies, provide them with appropriate contact procedures, if they do not hear from you and suspect an emergency has occurred

- **Consider deferring your travel plans** if you have a medical condition which could present problems for you or others while traveling

- **If you or your family require life sustaining medication** or other special supplies, ensure you carry a supply sufficient for your trip, plus a minimum reserve

of seven days extra, if possible

- **If a pet is traveling with you**, ensure that you have a supply of food, water, and other necessities for your pet as well

- **Carry a sufficient supply of money or travelers checks** with you for at least several days basic expenses

  - If a major emergency occurs and you are stranded on shore in an affected area, a bank or banking machine may not be easily accessible

While traveling to your destination via boat

- **Keep constant track of children, guests and pets,** as they could fall overboard and need to be rescued

- **Update your marine weather forecasts on a regular basis**, to ensure you are aware of the latest conditions. Consider altering your travel plans accordingly, if severe weather conditions are forecast or have developed

- **Ensure that you and any passengers avoid situations, or conditions that could lead to dehydration**, hunger, heat or sunstroke, hypothermia or extreme fatigue. Take appropriate actions to mitigate these conditions, if they do occur

PREPAREDNESS FOR OUTDOOR ACTIVITIES

Activities like camping, hiking or biking in remote areas can be pleasurable experiences, allowing us to enjoy the beauty of nature. However, the same reasons which draw us to a remote site (eg. solitude away from civilization) also cut us off from readily available resources, which we take for granted as part of our everyday lives, including convenient areas with shelter, heat, water, food and electricity.

Medical services may not be readily available if an injury occurs. Even the most seasoned camper, with state of the art equipment, could be subject to numerous potential hazards which can destroy, damage or sweep away equipment, including severe rainstorms, tornadoes, flash floods, fast moving water, wild animals or an accident.

In minutes, without warning, you may be stranded with limited resources, supplies and equipment. If you become lost or injured, or if an emergency occurs, you could be forced to rely on the limited resources at hand to survive while waiting for rescue or attempting to return safely to a familiar location.

It is therefore important to undertake a little emergency preparedness, as it relates to the outdoors.

 ## Supplies and equipment

Individuals who intend to travel in a remote area, to camp hike or bike should consider carrying at least a basic kit of emergency supplies in the event that an emergency occurs. You may be carrying the best equipment, with everything you need, however, an accident, which sinks your canoe with your pack, or an incident where a wild animal destroys your equipment, could leave you many days away from civilization with limited resources.

In addition to other camping supplies you may be carrying, a basic portable emergency kit for camping could include:

- **A working compass**
- **Regular matches** in a waterproof case, waterproof matches or other fire starting supplies (eg. flint and steel)
- **A flashlight with spare batteries**, or a flashlight with an alternate power source
- **A knife and/or axe**
- **A flexible saw**
- **Needle and thread**
- **An emergency blanket** (Mylar type)
- **Emergency candles**
- **Snare wire**
- **A plastic or metal mirror** which can be used for signaling (not glass)
- **Signal mirror, whistle** or other long distance signalling device
- **Water purification tablets**
- **A small supply of energy bars** or other similar non-perishable food supplies
- **Fishing line and fish hooks**

⊚ **A basic first aid kit**

⊚ **A supply of needed medications**, in a water proof case

Consider carrying smaller items for your emergency camping kit in a waterproof fanny pack or belly pack, separate from your backpack or other gear. At a minimum, each person who is on the camping trip should carry a separate basic emergency kit with them at all times, in the event they experience an accident or become lost, disoriented, or separated from the others.

One of the biggest concerns in an emergency which occurs in a remote area is remaining warm and dry. If possible, carry at least one change of spare clothing, socks, gloves, hat and other necessary gear, based on conditions, in a waterproof bag, knapsack or pack.

More advanced equipment is also available for outdoor activities, which can assist greatly in an outdoor emergency.

As an example, with the arrival of cheap available radio communication technology, personal communication radios have become widely available.

With ranges of 2 to 3 kilometres (1-2 miles) they can provide a ready communication source within their range of operation. Communicators of this nature may help you find other members of your group, if an individual becomes lost or separated.

Easily portable handheld Global Positioning System (GPS) units are also readily available now, to take on a camping trip. They can provide accurate coordinate information for any location in the world, by accessing information from satellites orbiting the earth.

Information from a GPS unit can help greatly in determining your position, in relation to the GPS coordinates for the position where you started. As a precaution, ensure you always take a reading at the beginning of your trip.

If you are carrying a GPS unit and/or a personal communicator with you on a trip, carry these items in a waterproof container or case. Also consider carrying spare batteries with you for these units, also in a waterproof container. If power supplies are low, turning these items on only when necessary can help conserve battery life.

Small, lightweight portable solar panels are also readily available, which may be used to power small devices such as a personal communicator or GPS on an emergency basis, or to charge spare batteries throughout the trip.

Prior to your trip, ensure all needed resources are present in your emergency camping kit and are in good condition. Repair or replace any necessary resources as required. If you require medication, ensure you carry a supply sufficient for your trip plus a reserve, (rule of thumb – a minimum of seven days extra supply, in addition to your requirements for the trip, if possible).

 Survival skills and information

Our increasing reliance on advanced technology to solve any problem has created an illusionary sense of comfort and security when we undertake outdoor activities, especially in remote areas. We go camping, hiking, mountain biking or skiing for fun, not expecting that an emergency or accident can occur without warning.

Like emergency preparedness for any other situation you are involved in, having the necessary information to make informed decisions for outdoor activities is critical for survival.

Consider taking a basic survival course, to better prepare yourself for emergencies which could occur outdoors. Courses of this nature are offered by many organizations and camping clubs throughout the country. More advanced courses are also available, to teach camping survival skills for winter conditions, canoeing, mountaineering and other specialty areas.

Consider taking a basic course in orienteering and map reading, in addition to a survival course. Many people have a compass in their emergency kit, but are unaware of how to use it properly in an emergency. An orienteering course can teach the necessary basic skills to navigate properly, using a compass and map as your guide.

Before any trip into a remote area, consider obtaining specific maps for the area you will be traveling in, and carry them with you. Many good camping maps are available for recognized federal, provincial and state parks, as well as affiliates of organizations like the Canadian Automobile Association (CAA) or the American Automobile Association (AAA). Map stores and government agencies normally carry, or can order, National Topographic System (NTS) maps published by Natural Resources Canada and the U.S. Geological Survey (USGS), in 1/250,000 scale and 1/25,000 scale, which cover most of North America.

Useful telephone numbers and web sites

CANADA
Natural Resources Canada – Canada Map Office

Web site
http://www.ccg-gcc.gc.ca/obs-bsn/equipment_e.htm
(map dealers)
http://maps.nrcan.gc.ca/search/index.html
(map on-line search)

Centre for Topographical Information
1-800-465-6277 E-mail: obs-bsn@dfo-mpo.gc.ca

UNITED STATES
U.S. Geological Survey (USGS)

Web site
http://edcsns17.cr.usgs.gov/EarthExplorer/
(map on-line search)
Customer Service – EROS Data Centre: 1-800-252-4547
                                                                          1-605-594-6933
                              E-mail: custserv@usgs.gov

If you are planning to use a GPS unit while camping, familiarize yourself with its proper use, and practice using it prior to your trip, as you may be unaware of many of the more complex functions it can perform. Using your GPS properly may prevent you from getting lost, and many save your life in an emergency!

Once you arrive at the trailhead or starting point for your journey, **consider taking a reading of the GPS coordinates for your starting point, to provide a reference point if you become lost or an emergency occurs.**

As with any other emergency preparedness activity, **consider taking a course in basic first aid, as well as a course in cardiopulmonary resuscitation (CPR).** Your skills in first aid may save a life, if an emergency involving injuries does occur.

 ## Communicate where you are

One of the most critical items of emergency preparedness for outdoor activities is <u>**to tell someone where you will be going**</u>. If a rescue or search needs to be initiated, having a starting point will greatly assist in this task, especially if time may be critical.

If you are planning to travel to a remote area on a camping or hiking trip, you should:

⊚ **Leave information** regarding your plans with a responsible individual, preferably in the form of a written note

⊚ **Give some details as to your itinerary,** including the date when you will be leaving, and when you plan to return, as well as a general description of where you are planning to camp or hike

⊚ **If you are planning to camp or hike in a remote location** in a federal, provincial or state park, inform park personnel that you will be in the park and give them a general idea as to where you will be camping or hiking. Inform them of when you plan to return

⊚ **If no park personnel are available**, consider leaving details of your itinerary in a trailhead log or in a location near the trailhead, if possible. If no other spot is available, leave an itinerary in a waterproof container, in an easily accessible location on your vehicle

If the individuals who are informed of your trip are unfamiliar with the area where you are camping, tell them whom they need to inform, if you do not return at the specified time. Provide them with appropriate emergency contact information for the area you are planning to travel in.

 ## Monitor weather conditions

Prior to leaving for a trip outdoors, monitor the weather conditions for the area you are traveling in, to determine if any specific weather warnings have been issued for that area.

If the trip is of extended duration (eg. more than a day), determine whether any severe weather conditions are occurring or warnings have been issued for surrounding areas, and whether they can affect your trip. Large weather systems can travel hundreds of kilometers (miles) and can affect a widespread area.

If severe weather is expected or is occurring, consider postponing your trip until conditions improve. The best way to prevent a potential emergency condition is to avoid the conditions, which can cause one to occur.

 ## During your outdoor trip

⊚ **Consider going on your trip with others**. In an emergency, two or more individuals are better than one

- **Heed any warnings** posted at trailheads, along a trail, or near unsafe areas. Ignoring danger warnings increases the risk of an emergency condition occurring. Report any unusual conditions you encounter or observe to park personnel or other officials, to protect the safety of others

- **Avoid contact with wildlife** that may pose a danger to you or others. Report any unusual wildlife behaviour you encounter or observe to appropriate officials in the area, to protect the safety of others

- **During a heavy rainfall,** and after heavy rainfall has occurred, avoid natural drainage areas to prevent being caught in a flash flood

- **Avoid crossing watercourses** that are more than knee deep for any of your group

- **In a narrow canyon or valley,** if you are intending to hike or undertake other activities, monitor weather conditions <u>upstream</u> of any rivers or creeks, to avoid being caught in a flash flood

  - **Rain does not have to be heavy or occur quickly to cause a flash flood.** Steady rain can build up the volume of water present in a watercourse. A dam or log jam may be dislodged, releasing water which has accumulated behind it

- **In cold weather with potentially high wind chills,** monitor conditions carefully and do not over-extend yourself. Carry extra warm clothing with you. Consider heading back immediately, and well in advance of any problems, if conditions become too severe

- **In thaw conditions, or in conditions where freezing and thawing have occurred regularly,** avoid traveling on ice on a lake or watercourse, as the ice may look intact, but may be thin or may have many air pockets. Insufficient load bearing capacity may be present to support your weight or the weight of equipment or vehicles

⊚ **Watch for any indication of potential emergency conditions,** which could occur (eg. water rising, dark clouds, glow at night which may indicate a forest fire, etc.). Take appropriate preventative measures, based on conditions

 ## When camping overnight

When stopping overnight in a remote location to camp, consider the following items of emergency preparedness when picking your campsite:

⊚ **Camp close enough to water for easy access**, but not close enough to be swept away if a flash flood occurs. Avoid potential floodplains or flat areas immediately beside a watercourse, where water can rise quickly

⊚ **Camp on higher ground** if possible, with adequate shelter. Avoid camping in canyons, small valleys or other low lying areas where water can be channeled

⊚ **Avoid camping in areas where trees or other debris can topple** or fall in high winds

⊚ **Determine an escape route**, if you must leave your campsite quickly, and plan an alternate escape route. Avoid camping in areas where you may be cut off from escaping easily or safely

⊚ **Avoid leaving open food, litter, trash, loose**

containers or gear scattered around the campsite when not in immediate use, as this may attract wildlife. Avoid keeping food, trash or litter in a tent. Store unused food and other supplies inside a vehicle or consider tying unused food and supplies in a bundle and storing it well above the ground, suspended between two trees, if possible

◉ **Control any open fires at all times,** and use camping stoves in a safe manner, to prevent the possibility of vegetation in the surrounding area igniting and causing a forest fire

TRAVEL PREPAREDNESS – OTHER COUNTRIES

We all dream of traveling to other countries, and many of us do so, either for holidays or for business reasons.

While travel to other countries can be a pleasurable experience, we must realize that other societies may have different laws and customs that we could be unfamiliar with, and different ways of doing things.

Services that we take for granted in our country may be unavailable in other countries, for short or extended periods of time. Or, in some cases, may not be available at all.

Many conflicts or potential conflicts, weather related conditions, natural disasters, and wide spread medical emergencies occur daily around the world. We must therefore be personally prepared for an emergency at any time while traveling.

 ## Prior to traveling to other countries

⊚ **Find out if travel is safe** both to, and around the countries you are visiting

The best way to avoid an emergency in a foreign country is not to place yourself at risk in the first place.

The area you are thinking of traveling to may have issues related to security, terrorism, medical outbreaks, natural disasters or other potential emergency situations which may be occurring on a one time or an on-going basis. As a result, government agencies may advise against travel to these countries completely, or for a set period of time.

Federal government agencies, in most countries, publish travel advisories related to other countries, which are updated frequently. They may also be accessed via phone or on the Internet. If travel is not recommended to the area you are planning to go to, consider postponing your trip until conditions improve.

Due to the continuing presence of various serious diseases, which are indigenous to certain countries, health officials may also advise you to receive specific inoculations prior to traveling to your destination, or to take certain medications while you are staying in the country in question. Specific requirements are usually based on the location you are traveling to and the length of time you are planning to stay.

Advice can be obtained from your doctor or from medical officials, in your local area, specializing in travel health. To ensure required immunizations are obtained and are current, consider contacting these officials at least six to eight weeks prior to travel, if possible.

Useful telephone numbers and web sites

CANADA
Government of Canada – Consular Affairs

Country Travel Reports / General Information
Web site
http://www.voyage.gc.ca/dest/index.asp
(English or French)
1-800-267-8376 (within Canada) or (613) 944-4000

Government of Canada – Health Canada

Travel Medical Program – Travel Health Advisories
Web site
http://www.hc-sc.gc.ca/pphb-dgspsp/tmp-pmv/pub_
e.html (English)
http://www.hc-sc.gc.ca/pphb-dgspsp/tmp-pmv/pub_f.html
(French)

Local government Travel Clinics are located in many areas
across Canada – refer to the web site(s) above for a listing of
clinics in your province.

UNITED STATES
U.S. Department of State – Bureau of Consular Affairs

Country Travel Reports / General Information
Web site
 http://travel.state.gov/
1-888-407-4747 (in the U.S.) or (317) 472-2328

National Centre for Infectious Diseases (CDC)

Travel Health Advisories
Web Site – http://www.cdc.gov/travel/
1-877-FYI-TRIP (394-8747)

⊚ **Do some research about the culture and customs
of the country you will be traveling to**. Be informed
of any potential legal differences between your country
or society, and the country in question. Traveling to
foreign countries means respecting foreign customs,
cultures and laws, even if they differ from what you are
accustomed to in your own country

Advance knowledge and preparation can prevent misunderstandings or legal problems with foreign officials. Contact the embassy or consulate of the country you are planning to visit in advance of your trip. If you have questions regarding laws, customs, or restrictions, these embassies will be able to help you.

- **Find out whether a VISA is required to enter any countries you plan to visit**. When you arrive, you may be refused entry into that country if a visa has not been obtained in advance, even if your passport is valid for your own country

NOTE:

Some countries also require that your passport be valid for six months or more past your date of entry, and may refuse you entry if your passport is due to expire within six months of your departure.

Check general information and travel reports published by your government for the country in question, to ensure that you meet their specific requirements prior to traveling.

- **Consider obtaining travel health insurance** for every person traveling with you. Medical insurance packages are available for travel to most countries in the world

This insurance may be obtained from a variety of sources including travel agencies, financial institutions and motor vehicle associations such as affiliates of the Canadian Automobile Association (CAA) or American Automobile Association (AAA) in North America.

Insurance of this nature is relatively inexpensive, and may be taken out for a specific trip or on a yearly basis, valid for multiple trips per year.

Remember, if you become ill in another country, medical coverage in your country may not cover the costs of necessary medical treatment. Even when traveling from Canada to the United States for a short period of time, medical costs can run into the thousands or tens of thousands of dollars if you require treatment. **Without insurance, you may be personally liable for all medical costs incurred.**

◉ **If you have a critical or life threatening medical condition,** ensure that proper facilities are available in the country where you are traveling, in case you need treatment for your condition. If you take life saving medications on a regular basis, find out whether you can obtain these medications in the country you are traveling to, and whether a prescription from a local doctor is required in that country, if additional medication is needed in an emergency

◉ **Leave important information regarding your travel plans** with a responsible relative or friend

◉ **Leave a photocopy of the identification page of your passport**

◉ **Provide a copy of your travel itinerary and contact information**, if this is available, to allow the responsible person to communicate with you or track your movements if an emergency occurs. Communicate with them, and inform them of any significant changes to the itinerary as necessary

◉ **Arrange a method of obtaining additional currency** from home or other sources, if money is lost or stolen

Find the local emergency contact number for your credit card company and/or contact number for obtaining replacement traveler's checks or credit cards, if these items are lost or stolen

Emergency travel supplies and equipment

 Travel emergency kit

Some supplies and equipment to consider for a travel emergency kit include:

⊚ **A flashlight with spare batteries**, or a flashlight with an alternate power source

⊚ **An emergency blanket** (eg. portable Mylar blanket)

⊚ **At least a basic first aid kit,** for longer trips, especially in areas where services or supplies may not be available, consider including:

- **Basic pain relief medication** such as Acetaminophen (Tylenol), Ibuprofen (Advil) and/or Aspirin in the original bottles (For other specific medications, see "Medications" section below)

- **Basic over the counter antihistamine medication**, to relieve allergies and inflammation

- **Basic anti nausea/motion sickness medication**

- **Basic anti-diarrhea medication**

- **Laxative medication, as required**

NOTE:

Consult with your doctor, prior to buying or putting together a travel first aid kit, to ensure all basic medications in your kit are compatible with any specific medications you are currently taking or medical conditions you may have.

Include or substitute specific prescription medications in place of those listed above, as recommended by your doctor, as required for your medical conditions.

- **Bandages** of assorted sizes
- **4-6 sterile gauze pads** (2 inch, 4 inch)
- **1-2 triangular sterile triangular cloth bandages**
- **1-2 rolls sterile roll bandages** (2 inch, 3 inch)
- **Fabric adhesive tape**
- **Pre-moistened antiseptic towelettes**
- **Scissors**
- **Tweezers**
- **Antibiotic ointment**
- **Soap**
- **An approved first aid manual** or handbook
- **Fasteners such as safety pins**
- **Any other first aid related items** you may wish to carry while traveling, based on your specific needs

- **Insect repellent containing DEET**, as required
- **Sunscreen**, with a protection factor of at least Sun Protection Factor 30 (SPF 45 or more for best protection), as required
- **An extra pair of prescription eyeglasses** as required

Also consider procuring a comfortable body belt or pouches, or other secure containers where valuable documents and additional financial resources can be carried under clothing.

 ## Medications

⊚ **Take a supply of medications for existing medical conditions** sufficient for your personal needs, for the entire travel period, plus an extra emergency supply if you are delayed (rule of thumb – at least 50% extra supply, if on a long trip)

NOTE:

Drugs that are legal and readily available without prescription in your country may be illegal or require a prescription in another country. If you are unsure of the status of drugs you take on a regular basis, contact the consulate or embassy for the country you are planning to travel to.

Drugs you are carrying may come under intense scrutiny by foreign officials. Carry over the counter drugs in their original packages, and carry prescription drugs in their original properly labeled bottles. Carry a copy of your prescription, listing both the trade and generic names of the drugs.

Consider obtaining a doctor's note describing why you are taking the drugs being carried.

⊙ **Take other medical supplies required to administer your medications**, in sufficient quantity to last for your entire trip, plus an extra emergency supply (rule of thumb – at least 50% extra supply for a long trip)

NOTE:

If you must carry sterile syringes and needles for your medical condition, ensure that you obtain a recognized medical certificate that states they are for medicinal use. In countries with drug trafficking problems, a traveler found carrying syringes without explanation, may face serious legal difficulties with police authorities.

- **If you are carrying essential medications and supplies with you**, divide your supplies among two or more pieces of luggage, so that if one piece is lost, delayed or stolen in transit, alternate supplies are still available

Information

- **Carry a photocopy of the identification page of your passport**, in a location separate from your actual passport

- **Carry an information page listing your credit card numbers, traveler's check numbers** and other appropriate financial information in a separate secure location other than your wallet

- **Carry information related to your medical history** with you in an easily accessible location, if you suffer from specific medical conditions, as a reference source for foreign physicians in a medical related emergency

During Your Trip

While traveling in a foreign country ...

- **Know the type of emergencies, which may occur in the country** or area where you will be traveling. If you are unclear as to what conditions may occur, seek advice from individuals in the location where you will be staying

- **Learn the meaning of any specific emergency related signals** (eg. horns, sirens, buzzers, etc.) and what to do in an emergency if the signal occurs

- **Advise the location or person you will be staying with of any special needs or disabilities you may have.** Tell them the help you will need if an emergency occurs

- **Know the location and contact information for your country's embassy** or consulate, and carry this information with you at all times. Carry a supply of spare change (specific to the country you are in) tokens, or other specific items which may be required if you need to make a phone call quickly

- **Do not walk alone in remote areas,** back streets or beaches where there may be risk of attack, assault, theft or purse snatching

- **Leave your valuables back home when traveling abroad,** to avoid having them stolen or store valuables in a hotel safe when not in use

- **Do not carry all your traveler's checks and currency with you,** if possible. Store currency which is not needed for each day's use in a secure and safe location

- **Consider carrying some of your daily supply of currency in a location which you can easily access** (eg. pocket, belt pouch), and carry an additional emergency supply in a concealed money belt or pouch

- **If you have more than one credit card,** consider storing or carrying one card in a secure separate location from your wallet or purse, for emergency purposes

189

⊚ **Avoid specific foods and water directly from taps,** wells or other sources, if recommended to do so by travel health authorities in your own country, to limit diarrhea related or other problems. Try to obtain bottled water or other beverages only from reputable sources. Avoid using ice cubes, which may have been produced directly from tap water sources

⊚ **Take any travel related medications** required for the area you will be visiting (eg. anti-malaria pills) on a set schedule, as recommended by the travel health authority in your country

⊚ **Use recommended insect repellants** regularly, especially at dusk or dawn, in areas where they are required, to limit the possibility of contracting insect transmitted diseases

⊚ **Wash your hands frequently**, and always before eating, to limit the possibility of contracting any diseases transmitted by touch

⊚ **Wear appropriate clothing**, for hot weather or cold weather travel conditions. Use layered clothing if possible and as required, so you can add or remove as necessary

⊚ **Take appropriate precautions to avoid heat exhaustion**, heat stress or other hot weather related conditions (see advice under "If a Hot Weather Emergency Occurs" under "Emergency Preparedness for the Home")

PREPAREDNESS FOR SPECIAL NEEDS

Special needs can apply to a variety of conditions that we deal with in our lives.

These needs may be physical in nature, limiting mobility, or preventing an individual from undertaking specific activities, which may include caring for their personal needs. Special needs may be mental in nature, limiting cognitive function, or limiting the ability to make informed decisions.

Special needs may also be medical in nature, requiring specialized care to be undertaken or medications to be taken on a regular basis, to prevent the deterioration of a condition, or a life-threatening situation.

In some cases, all the conditions described above may contribute to the special needs of an individual. A person may be born with these needs, or acquire the need for assistance, due to an accident, disease, age or infirmity. In certain special needs cases, we may also have to provide a life support environment for others as part of our normal activities.

Infants also rely on parents to nurture, feed and protect them from harm, until they are grown. Domestic animals kept as pets, working animals and livestock rely on human intervention on a regular basis to survive.

The special needs situations listed above are only some of the situations which could represent specific and special challenges in an emergency, as normal support mechanisms may be disrupted for a short term or for an extended period of time. It is therefore important to consider special needs as part of emergency preparedness activities.

Personal assessment for special needs

If your household contains individuals with special needs, or you are planning on behalf of someone outside your household with special needs, you may wish to undertake a personal assessment. This should be done in addition to the normal pre-planning efforts described previously (See "Where to Start"). You may also wish to undertake a personal assessment for other situations where pets or any animals are involved, or any other special situations you can think of.

A personal assessment does not have to be detailed or complex, but it should be a realistic review of your capabilities or the capabilities of the person(s) you are planning for. By doing an assessment, it will allow you to better plan and prepare specifically for any special needs requirements, if an emergency does occur.

Some items to consider as part of the personal assessment could include, as appropriate:

⊙ **What specific severe or mild disabilities are involved** and what challenges might these pose?

⊙ **What personal care needs are required regularly?** (eg. physical, medical, other). How could these be affected by an emergency?

⊙ **What personal care equipment is required on a regular basis?** How might this equipment be affected in an emergency (eg. a power disruption)? If this equipment was unavailable, what alternatives are available?

⊙ **What personal assistance is required on a regular basis** to address these special needs? If normal caregivers are unavailable in an emergency, who can provide temporary assistance (eg. administer medicines, assist in dressing, etc.)?

◉ **Are other people aware of your special needs or the needs of someone in your care,** in your apartment block or multiple person condominium development? Would it be known that you or someone in your care could require additional assistance in an emergency? Is a signaling method available to convey an emergency if normal communications systems are unavailable? How would this signal be communicated to others?

◉ **How would you or the person in your care evacuate a building** in an emergency? What assistance would be required? What personal mobility aids would be required? What could be done if normal mobility aids are unavailable?

◉ **How would you or the person under your care know that an emergency is occurring** based on the special needs involved? Who would inform you or them, if an emergency were imminent?

◉ **What pets, working animals, livestock or other animals, are present in the household** or are part of your activities or those of the disabled person's activities? How would these animals be affected by an emergency? What considerations might be present related to caring for these animals in an emergency?

Answers to appropriate questions above, or other questions related to additional specific needs should be listed and considered as part of your emergency planning efforts.

Personal emergency plan for special needs

Based on your personal assessment described previously, consider preparing a personal emergency plan directly related to the special requirements in your household, or for any special needs of person(s) in your care. Consider keeping a copy of the plan in an easily accessible location in the home (eg. in an emergency kit), and distributing a copy to each member of a support network, if one has been created (see "Support Networks" under various special needs sections below).

Every personal emergency plan will be different, but should be as brief and concise as possible. It should be tailored to the particular special requirements of the individual or situation. Information in a personal emergency plan could include, as appropriate:

Emergency information

⊙ **The names of all individuals in a support network**, along with their telephone numbers and addresses (See individual sections on "Support Networks" below)

⊙ **Information related to relatives** or other individuals who may need to be contacted in an emergency

⊙ **The location(s) of a spare key for the home**, which is held by a trusted individual, or in some other location. Include the location of vehicle or other keys necessary to operate special equipment as required

- The location of **emergency supplies**, medications, special equipment and reference information (eg. equipment manuals or special instructions)

Medical information

- **Birth date for the individual** (may be required for hospital admission if the person is unconscious)

- **A brief description of the capabilities of the person** and potential care needs, as well as instructions on how best to assist them in an emergency

- **A description of any areas of the person's body which may have reduced feeling,** if injuries have occurred and they cannot check these areas themselves

- **A listing of specific medical conditions that the person may suffer from,** and medications taken, including dosages and a schedule of when the medications need to be taken

- **A listing of any allergy sensitivities, or reactions to medication,** if hospitalization is required on an emergency basis, and you or the person being cared for cannot communicate

- **A listing of any special dietary requirements** related to the special needs involved

- **A listing of the style and type of pacemaker which a person uses,** if required, including serial number

- **A listing of the style and type of other medical devices,** including serial numbers

- A listing of the location and address of life sustaining facilities that are used on a regular basis (eg. dialysis facilities), and the frequency of treatment. Also list alternate locations for treatment in the area where the individual lives

- Contact number(s) for doctors who treat any specific medical condition(s)

- Special information (eg. religious beliefs, other special requirements) which may affect treatment

- Photocopies of health insurance cards, Medicare cards or medical insurance documentation (depending on the country or your residence)

 Evacuation plan

- A brief description of the person's needs, and any assistance which will be required if they have to evacuate a specific location (eg. home, office, or other locations they frequent regularly

- A listing of evacuation routes which may be used to exit from a specific location (eg. home, office, or other)

- A description of the location where devices are stored which may be required to assist the individual in an evacuation

- A written listing of any special instructions which emergency responders or personnel unfamiliar with the condition of the person with special needs will need in order to assist them in performing the evacuation safely

Typical examples can include:

- **"Please take my oxygen supply, and medications from the refrigerator,** if safe to do so, as I need these to survive"
- **"Please do not attempt to straighten my legs.** They are fused in a bent position"
- **"I am legally blind, and require guidance.** Please allow me to grasp your arm firmly"
- **"I require an artificial speech device to communicate.** Please take this device with me, if safe to do so"
- **"I have a learning impairment.** Please write down important instructions"

⊚ **A written description of any priority needs,** which may be necessary in an evacuation, if the person's condition does not allow them to wait in line for food, water or other assistance

Support network for special needs

In many situations, relatives or personal friends may not be immediately available to provide support to persons with special needs, if an emergency occurs at home.

Many individuals live in locations away from elderly or disabled relatives or friends, and therefore must travel a distance to be of assistance. Work activities or lifestyle activities may also prevent families or friends from being available on a temporary or regular basis. If this is the case, consider creating a personal support network consisting of nearby relatives, friends and other individuals who could be available to assist the person as required.

People who may be able to participate as part of a personal support network could include:

- **Trusted neighbours** in the immediate vicinity

- **Roommate(s)**

- **Trusted co-worker(s)**

- **Trusted members of a church**, to which you or the person belongs

- **Trusted members of other associations** or organizations to which you or the person belongs

- **Local officials**, if living in a small town

- **Home health care agencies**

- **Other trusted individuals**

Try to get a number of individuals to assist in a personal support network at home, as one individual may be away at certain times, due to work related activities, holidays, or other activities. As a rule of thumb, try to get at least three individuals if possible, to assist in the personal support network.

Members of a support network should live reasonably close to the person's residence. It is preferable to have individuals in the immediate area or in the same building, for multi-person dwellings, to allow them to provide assistance within a short period of time. As an alternate, consider individuals who are outside of the immediate area, but live locally, who drive and have regular access to a vehicle, to allow them to respond to a situation quickly.

First aid training, and training in cardiopulmonary resuscitation techniques (CPR) is an asset. If possible, try to get at least one individual who has taken this training to participate as part of the support network.

Also consider extending the personal support network to the workplace, and other locations the person with special needs frequents on a regular basis. Most workplaces have emergency plans that require them to identify individuals with special needs within a facility. Consider discussing your special requirements, or the needs of the person you are planning for, with the person in charge of safety or emergency preparedness in the workplace.

Consider preparing a personal emergency plan directly related to the special needs for the person under consideration, including emergency information, medical information, evacuation information or other special concerns, as appropriate. (See the Personal Emergency Plan for Special Needs section above, for suggestions). Distribute a copy to each individual in the personal support network. Also consider keeping a copy of the plan in an easily accessible location in the home (eg. in an emergency kit).

If a personal emergency plan has not been created, at least consider storing a brief written summary of critical information for the person in an accessible location. Include contacts and critical medical information, as required. Provide this information to each member of the personal support network. (See "Emergency Information" and "Medical Information" under "Personal Emergency Plan for Special Needs").

If a person is willing to volunteer to be part of the support network, ensure that they have the required information to be able to assist in an emergency, and ensure they feel comfortable with their responsibilities. Some items to consider include:

- **Introducing them to other individuals in the support network**, if they are not already acquainted

- **Introducing them to relatives or others** they may need to contact in an emergency

- **Showing them normal storage locations** for information, equipment and supplies

- **Teaching them how to operate necessary equipment**

- **Teaching them how to communicate with the individual**, if special communication is required

- **Teaching them how to deal with any specific cognitive or behavioral disabilities**

- **Teaching them how to deal with any other specific age related conditions**

- **Teaching them how to safely move any equipment** used for a disability

- Teaching them how to administer necessary medications, in proper dosage

- Teaching them how to properly transfer the person being planned for to another location, if they are immobile and cannot be moved without assistance

- Making sure that any service animal being used is familiar with members of the support network, in case the animal needs to be cared for by other members of the group

Have them practice with any special equipment, to make them feel more confident with its use. Consider taping instructions to the equipment, possibly as a laminated plastic card, for easy reference if they need to refresh their memory in an emergency.

Members of a support network should be encouraged to remain in contact with each other on a regular basis, to share important information as required. If they suspect an emergency has occurred, they should be encouraged to seek assistance and support from other members of the network, if required.

Members of the support network should also establish procedures and schedules between themselves and the person involved, to ensure that the person is contacted on a regular basis, to determine they are safe and that no medical related conditions or accidents have occurred.

Discuss how the person involved will communicate with the individuals in the support network in an emergency, and arrange an appropriate check-in procedure. If telephones are unavailable, arrange an alternate check-in method to determine whether assistance is required.

Also consider developing a procedure with the members of the support network, for providing immediate notification to the individual, when a major emergency has occurred, and sharing any other important information. This is especially important if the specific disability the person has prevents normal signals from being seen or heard.

If the person with special needs is planning to travel, and will be away for a period of time, ensure the support network is informed. Also let them know when the person can be expected back, and contact them if plans change for any reason.

Ensure relatives or personal friends who live in other areas are given the names of the individuals in the support network, along with their addresses and telephone numbers. If they experience unusual circumstances (eg. no answer to regular phone calls), they should be instructed to contact members of the support network closest to the person with special needs, to check to see if there is a problem.

Emergency preparedness for infants and children

Infants and young children are totally reliant on their parents or other caregivers for support in normal everyday activities. In an emergency, the same support is needed, to allow them to survive and prosper.

In addition to support required for normal growth and development, infants may suffer from other congenital conditions due to problems during pregnancy, genetic defects, premature birth, or diseases and physical conditions acquired after birth. Even older children without requirements for direct support may feel special forms of distress in an emergency. You, as a responsible adult, may feel helpless and fearful in the face of a major emergency. For a child, these feelings may seem overwhelming.

Where infants and children are involved, it is essential to undertake some specific emergency preparedness activities.

 ## Supplies and equipment

In addition to the items, which are outlined in other sections for preparedness in the home, vehicles or other situations, consider having the following extra supplies on hand for emergencies involving infants or young children:

- **Spare diapers** and other related supplies

- **Non-perishable infant food supplies** and formula, especially any special food items required. Food supplies requiring limited preparation, and which do not require heating are best in an emergency situation

- **Non-perishable juice boxes** or other drinks

- **A supply of any required life sustaining medications** which are administered regularly

Consider stockpiling supplies of these items, sufficient for at least three days of use, preferably a week. Consider having on hand at least 9 litres (two gallons) of clean water per day for drinking, cleaning and other purposes for infants and young children.

For all children, consider your choice of foods when stockpiling food resources for emergency use. Consider nutritious choices of non-perishable foods that your children can and will eat (eg. canned fruits and puddings).

For your first aid kit, consider having supplies of any basic non-prescription medications required for your child (eg. painkillers) in child doses or formulas, for easy use in an emergency. If specific children's doses are unavailable, consider including a listing of proper children's doses of adult medications which may be safely administered.

Also consider stockpiling some supplies of favorite non-perishable comfort foods for use in an emergency. If evacuation is required, consider taking a favorite blanket or pillow and a supply of favorite toys, including soft huggable animal toys. The disruptions caused by an emergency, even on a temporary basis, can be stressful to children. Having even a small number of familiar comforts can go a long way towards making a child feel happier and safer.

 ## Information

As part of your emergency preparedness activities, get older children involved in the process. Many children say they feel safer if they are involved and know what to do if an emergency occurs.

Important items to explain to your children related to emergencies include:

- **What constitutes an emergency**
- **How to phone for help** in your community
- **When it is appropriate to phone for help** using an emergency number. Show them where the emergency contact phone numbers are posted or located in

your home, if they need to contact someone in an emergency

> NOTE:
>
> *Ensure that your children know that <u>phoning an emergency number is not a game!</u>*

On the basis of the emergencies which you have determined can occur in your area, talk to your children about what to do if a specific type of emergency occurs. Some items to discuss can include:

- **Showing them the safest location to go to**, if a tornado, earthquake, hurricane, or other major emergency occurs, as appropriate. Rehearse safety behaviours with your children. Talking about what to do is not enough

- **Teaching your children to recognize danger signals** (eg. smoke coming from a room) and what a fire alarm sounds like and means, and what to do if an alarm is activated. If your local area has community wide warning signals (eg. sirens), teach your children what these signals mean, and what to do

- **Informing your children of any personal emergency arrangements you have established and whom they should contact**, if you cannot be located in an emergency. Establish contacts that are both in your community, and outside your community, in the event of a major emergency that could affect your entire local area

It is best for your child if the person(s) being contacted are persons that they know well (eg. close relatives, neighbours, close family friends, etc.). Encourage them to phone the emergency contact, if they are scared and cannot contact you in an emergency.

Also discuss a meeting point with your children, where you will all go if you are separated and cannot go home in an emergency.

Provide them with an emergency contact card, if you have prepared one to carry in their knapsack, jacket or some other convenient location. Ensure appropriate emergency contact numbers, and meeting locations are listed (See the "Contact Points" section, page 62, for further information and a sample emergency contact card).

Ensure that any baby sitters or other temporary caregivers in your household are aware of your emergency contact procedures when you are away. Show them the location where your emergency contact listings are located or posted. Encourage them to contact you or your alternate personal emergency contacts, if you cannot be reached and an emergency has occurred in the household.

⊚ **Show your older, more responsible children the location of your family emergency kit.** Show them how to appropriately use any specialized supplies and equipment stored in the kit

Also inform temporary caregivers of any special needs or requirements that your infants or children may have. Show them the location where specialized equipment, foods or medicines are stored, as well as the proper way to use these supplies. Also show caregivers the location where your basic and specialized emergency supplies are stored, for use in an emergency while you are away.

 **Child proofing to prevent emergencies**

Children are constantly curious about the world around them, and will explore their world looking for interesting things to play with. In many cases, they will also attempt to imitate the behaviours of their parents or other adults. In their world, they do not consider that a situation may be dangerous or potentially fatal.

Children are also extremely trusting by nature. They do not consider that another person may intentionally cause them harm. A missing or abducted child is an emergency which can be extremely traumatic to parents as well as others involved.

Children do not have an innate sense of responsibility (this is hopefully learned in later life). As such, they may inadvertently cause an emergency situation to occur, because we as adults have undertaken some careless action. It is therefore important to protect your children from situations or actions that could have a negative affect on them, or others, as part of your emergency preparedness activities.

Some items to consider <u>in and around the home</u> include:

⊚ **Keeping matches and lighters** away from easy reach of children, locked up if possible

⊚ **Keeping knives and other sharp objects** out of the reach of children, and secured, if possible

⊚ **Keeping rifles, pistols and other firearms** unloaded and locked up

⊚ **Keeping common household chemicals** such as corrosives (eg. cleaning chemicals or detergents), flammables (eg.

solvents, lighters fluids, gasoline), and poisons (eg. insecticides, pesticides) out of easy reach of children, locked up if possible when not in use

- **Keeping prescription medicines** out of easy reach of children, in original tamper proof bottles, and locked up if possible

- **Making sure that young children are supervised** at all times, to ensure they are not left alone in potentially dangerous situations

Some items to consider <u>outside of the home</u> include:

- **Teaching children to recognize the sound of sirens** on emergency vehicles, and to go to the side of the road, and get off their bicycles or other transportation, if appropriate, until the emergency vehicles have gone past

- **Teaching children not to follow emergency vehicles**

- **Teaching children not to play far from home**, or away from familiar areas. Teach them not to venture into unfamiliar areas without your permission or supervision

- **Teaching children not to play near power lines** or other potentially dangerous electrical or mechanical devices

- **Teaching children to play away from dangerous locations** like construction areas, open excavations, cliffs or open bodies of water and storm water retention ponds, if they are not supervised

- **Teaching children not to play with strange or unfamiliar objects they may find**, and to tell you or another responsible adult about any unusual items they do find, as quickly as possible

- **Teaching children to report life threatening, dangerous, or unusual situations** to you or to some other responsible adult that they know, as quickly as possible

- **Teaching children to avoid contact with strangers**, especially if they are asked to go with them for whatever reason

- **Teaching children what to do if they become lost or disoriented**, based on where you live (eg. being lost in a forest, or in a part of a city they are not familiar with)

 In an actual emergency affecting your family...

- <u>**Most importantly, stay as calm as possible**</u>, based on the circumstances involved. Children are very sensitive to parent's or other adult's responses to the world around them, and will look to you for guidance as to how to react in the highly unusual circumstances of an emergency. Reacting with high levels of anxiety, alarm or stress yourself may make them more frightened or anxious

- **Turn off the TV,** except to receive updates, to restrict the amount of emergency related news coverage that your children watch

Even if you are not directly involved in a major emergency, children can become frightened when they see the same pictures from a major disaster being played over and over. Emergencies, which affect areas they are familiar with, may be especially traumatic.

Children have vivid imaginations. In the mind of a child, each time a picture is shown may represent a separate emergency occurring. As an example, during the World Trade Center bombing on September 11, 2001, many children became stressed by watching the continuous news coverage. When questioned, they thought that each time the planes crashed into the buildings, another disaster was occuring, due to the intensity of the coverage, and the same pictures being shown over and over.

⊚ **Be honest with your children** and explain what's going on. Base the amount of information you give them and the level of detail, on what is appropriate and manageable for their age level. Get down to their eye level when you talk to them

⊚ **Reassure your children and keep them informed.** Without your constant reassurances in an emergency, children's imaginations can run wild. Some of the most common fears children have can include:

- **They caused the emergency to occur**, by something they said or did wrong
- **The emergency event will happen again**, or won't ever stop
- **Everyone they love will be injured or killed** and they will be left alone
- **They will be separated from their family** or friends forever
- **They will never have a home again**

Items which adults might consider insignificant may be extremely significant to a child, due to the scope of their world (eg. loss of a favourite stuffed animal, special toy, or blanket, etc.). Try to be realistic but comforting in your reassurances, based on the events that have occurred, using your own experience in the emergency as a guide. Relate your own experiences in a way they can understand.

- **Listen to your children without judgement** and let them know they can have their own feelings about the situation. Encourage them to ask questions about the emergency. Tell them that they do not have to be "brave" or "tough", and that it is okay to cry, if necessary

- **Try to establish some routine** during and after the emergency. Emergency events are disruptive to adults but a child thrives on daily routine

Children can become anxious or worried when routines are disrupted. Try to establish some semblance of normality in the form of familiar comfort foods or some activities, which are familiar (eg. reading a favourite story), to keep your children relaxed, if possible. Let them have some control in decisions that personally affect them (eg. what clothes to wear, what foods to eat, etc.) within reason.

- **Monitor your children's behaviour after a major emergency is over.** Adults can experience delayed stress related conditions after a major emergency – children are susceptible to the same types of stresses, but may not be able to express their feelings in words

Some indicators of delayed stress in children could include:

- **Becoming easily upset**, for no apparent reason
- **Undergoing unusual personality changes** (eg. becoming noisy and aggressive when they were normally quiet and obedient)
- **Being afraid of sleeping alone**, when they did not have this problem previously
- **Reverting to younger behaviours** unusual for their age

- **Losing trust in adults**, because they could not prevent the emergency from occurring
- **Not wanting parents out of their sight**
- **Refusing to go to school** or other locations they used to enjoy

Children may need your help, or the support and understanding of others to deal with feelings resulting from an emergency.

After an emergency is over, involve your children. Give them chores to do, which are their personal responsibility, based on their capabilities. Making them part of the activities can go a long way towards helping in their own personal recovery process.

Emergency preparedness for the elderly

In a major emergency, elderly individuals may require additional considerations, due to their age, health, mental condition, or specific infirmities.

Also, because a medical emergency may occur at any time, special considerations may be required, especially if relatives, friends or other normal caregivers are not immediately available to provide support or comfort.

If you are elderly, or you wish to plan for emergency situations on behalf of an elderly individual, you may wish to consider some of the following items as part of your emergency preparedness activities.

 **Supplies and equipment**

In addition to the items, which are outlined in other sections for preparedness in the home, vehicles or other situations, consider having the following extra supplies on hand for emergency purposes, to be stored in your home or vehicle:

- **Extra eyeglasses**, as appropriate

- **Spare hearing aid batteries**, if one is used, based on the model and type of hearing aid

- **Extra batteries for a motorized wheelchair** or other special needs equipment

- **Extra canes, walkers** or other medical assistance devices, as required

- **A supply of life sustaining medications** sufficient for three days to a week of treatment, if these are taken on a regular basis

Talk to their doctor, or other specialty caregivers, to determine what specific supplies or equipment should be included in their emergency kit. If required, ensure that you or the elderly individual that you are planning for is supplied with, and wears a medic alert bracelet, which indicates any allergies or special conditions.

For elderly persons who are still in their homes and cannot be checked continuously, consider subscribing to a home based alert system. These systems include a device which is carried or worn and can be used to signal for help, if emergency assistance is required.

Emergency preparedness for a person with disabilities

In a major emergency, individuals with a disability may require additional considerations, due to their special needs. Also special considerations may be required, especially if normal caregivers are not immediately available to provide support or comfort.

If you have a disability, or you wish to plan for emergency situations on behalf of an individual with a disability, you may wish to consider some of the following items as part of your emergency preparedness activities.

 ## Supplies and equipment

In addition to the normal supplies and equipment in a basic emergency kit for home, vehicles or other locations, (see the appropriate sections previously described in this guide), you may wish to include extra items in your emergency kit for specific disabilities, as follows:

Possible extra supplies if you have a <u>visual disability or are blind</u>:

- ⊙ **A spare pair of prescription eyeglasses**, as appropriate

- ⊙ **An extra magnifier**, if required

- ⊙ **A battery powered talking clock**, Braille or large print clock and extra batteries, as required

- ⊙ **An extra cane**, to assist in navigating

◉ **Extra emergency supplies for a service animal**, as appropriate

Mark your emergency supplies appropriately, based on your particular needs, with fluorescent tape, Braille labels or large print labels, to allow them to be identified quickly in an emergency.

As an additional emergency preparedness measure, you may wish to consider marking shut-off valves in your home appropriately for easy identification, based on your particular needs, with fluorescent tape, Braille labels or large print labels.

Possible extra supplies if you have a <u>hearing loss or are deaf</u>:

◉ **A small portable battery operated television**, in the event that emergency instructions are provided via close captioning, American Sign Language, or other appropriate methods

◉ **An extra hearing aid** and spare batteries, as appropriate

◉ **Paper pads and pens/pencils**, for visual communications

◉ **A flashlight, whistle or noisemaker** and paper and pencils by your bed

◉ **A card in your basic emergency kit** and one with you at all times, indicating you are deaf and any other critical information (eg. "I do/do not understand American Sign Language" "I can/cannot read lips" "I have a service animal to assist me, who may legally remain with me", etc.)

Possible extra supplies if you have a <u>speech related communication disability</u>:

- **Paper pads and pencils / pens** for visual communications

- **A word or letter board and preprinted key phrases** you may need in an emergency

- **Spare charged batteries** for any specialized communications devices you may use

If you use a laptop computer to communicate, consider having a power inverter available in your emergency kit, which allows power from a DC power source such as a car battery to be converted into AC power, to run your laptop's charging adapter. A battery powered emergency power pack with a built-in AC inverter may also be used to provide additional DC or AC power for your computer for a limited time (see the section on New Age Emergency Preparedness for descriptions of power inverters, power packs and other special equipment).

Alternately, consider purchasing an additional laptop charging adapter which can be connected directly to a DC utility / cigarette lighter plug in a vehicle or other device.

NOTE:

If charging a laptop battery from a running vehicle in a garage, ensure that proper ventilation is present by opening the garage door, to prevent build-up of carbon monoxide or other toxic gases.

If you use a specialized communication device such as an electronic communicator or artificial larynx, consider having this device close at hand in a safe place at all times, if you need to leave your residence quickly in an emergency.

Possible extra supplies if <u>you are required to self-administer life sustaining medications</u>:

- ◎ **A two to three day supply of additional clean instruments**, supplies and equipment, as appropriate, to administer the medication

- ◎ **Spare batteries for specialized monitors** or other battery powered equipment

- ◎ **A document listing medications taken**, required dosage, and frequency required per day, week etc., as well as any special handling instructions if a stranger must administer your medication to you in an emergency

- ◎ **A document listing your doctor's name**, and contact information for obtaining additional life sustaining medication on an emergency basis

Possible extra supplies if you have a <u>learning or cognitive disability</u>:

- ◎ **An extra written or printed copy of any instructions or reference information** you normally need for everyday activities

- ◎ **A written or printed copy of any emergency instructions** you may need to assist you in an actual emergency

- ◎ **A paper pad and pencils/pens** to write down additional information or instructions as required

Write instructions and information in a form that you can easily understand, or remember in the confusion that could occur in an emergency, possibly as point form notes or step-by-step instructions.

Possible extra supplies if you use a <u>manually operated wheelchair</u>:

⊚ **A patch kit**, extra inner tubes and can of compressed air, to repair flat tires, if the tires are not puncture proof

⊚ **A pair of heavy gloves**, to use while moving about in your chair, as glass and other debris may be present on the floor, and could be picked up by the wheels

Possible extra supplies if you use a <u>motorized wheelchair, scooter or personal transporter</u>:

⊚ **An extra deep cycle battery**

   • **Car batteries of similar voltage** may be considered for use as a substitute, if absolutely necessary, but will not last as long as a battery made specifically for powering this equipment

⊚ **A portable charging system or emergency power pack**, which allows the wheelchair or scooter battery to be charged from another battery, or from the utility/cigarette plug-in in a vehicle

⊚ **A power inverter of sufficient capacity**, which would allow a normal charger to be plugged into a vehicle cigarette lighter or utility plug. (See the section on "New Age Emergency Preparedness" for a description of power inverters)

- **A lightweight manual wheelchair**, if your disability allows you to use one

Consider having these items available in storage, even if you are unable to change batteries or use the stored items yourself, based on your special needs, as other individuals may be able to assist you in an emergency.

Emergency preparedness for pets

One of the least planned aspects of emergency is preparedness for pets.

Like humans, your pet may become ill or injured on a weekend or holiday, and require emergency veterinary care if your regular veterinarian is unavailable.

House pets also rely on you totally to provide life support, in the way of food, sanitary arrangements, medicine and even emotional comfort. Pets, which live outdoors, still may not have the necessary skills to forage for food, and can be impacted by the same hazards that affect you in an emergency.

Pets left behind in an emergency may exit buildings through storm-damaged areas or broken windows, escape and become lost. Animals left to fend for themselves outdoors may suffer from exposure, starvation, and wild predators or consume contaminated food or water. Abandoning pets without some preparation, if you are required to evacuate your home, may be tantamount to condemning them to starvation, severe injury or death.

Due to the uncertainty of an emergency situation, you cannot just assume that you will be out of your home for a short period of time. You may be away for hours, days or even weeks, and may not be allowed to return for any reason. If you have a pet, some advance preparation may be necessary to prepare for their special needs.

While it is a good idea to evacuate your pet from the home when you leave, you may still be separated from your pet, even if it accompanies you. In a major emergency, government designated evacuation centres may not allow pets in the shelter, for space or health related reasons. If they do, they may require pets to be secured in carrier boxes or cages, or to be housed in a separate area from human evacuees.

Service animals required by persons with special needs, in most communities, are normally allowed to remain with them if they are required to be evacuated to a government-organized shelter.

However, consider contacting the appropriate emergency organization in your community to ensure that this is indeed the case. If required, consider having legal documentation related to your service animal remaining with you in an emergency, and include it for reference purposes in your basic emergency kit.

Supplies and equipment

In addition to the supplies and equipment in your basic emergency kit listed previously for homes and vehicles (see the appropriate sections described in this guide), you may wish to prepare an emergency kit for your pets as well.

Specific items in your pet's emergency kit would depend on the type of animal, and their particular needs. Some items to consider depending on the pet could include:

- **An extra leash**, harness or other necessary item to control your pet

- **An extra collar** with proper identification for each pet

- **A pet specific first aid book**, if available

- **A supply of life sustaining medications** your pet may require, in a water proof container

- **A supply of special needs medication**, if required (eg. pet Gravol or a required sedative, if your pet does not travel well)

- **An information sheet related to your pet**, in a waterproof bag (see the "Information" section below for suggestions on information to include)

- **A supply of non-perishable pet food** in sturdy containers sufficient for at least three days per pet (preferably a week). Consider packing any required perishable pet foods at the last minute, if you must evacuate your home

- **Food/water bowl(s)** for each pet

- **Cat litter** of the type used regularly (rule of thumb – sufficient for at least three days) and a litter box, as required

- **A small supply of favorite toys**, to reduce stress

- **Newspaper**

- **Paper towels**

- **Grooming items**

- **A manual can opener**, if required, and one is not already present in your emergency supplies

Try to keep all the items which form part of your pet's emergency kit in the same location, preferably in a sturdy bag or box, to ensure it remains together at all times. Make a list of the equipment and supplies, which should be present, and store it in the box as well or on the outside of the bag.

Consider itemizing any other items you think your pet may require in an evacuation on an evacuation checklist, and store this list with the kit as well.

If supplies are removed or used in the emergency kit, replace them as soon as possible.

Having an appropriate carrier or cage, of sufficient size to allow them to comfortably sit or move around, for each of your pets, is also a good idea. If your pet panics or attempts to flee due to anxiety, they will be securely and safely controlled.

If an evacuation is required, consider taking some of your pet's favourite items, which would not normally be present in the emergency kit, such as a favourite pet bed, towel or any items you think would help reduce stress when relocating in an emergency.

 Emergency information

To have permanent information on your dog or cat always present with them, consider having a microchip implanted or having your pet tattooed with an identification number.

Microchips are very small (roughly the size of the tip of a pencil) and are implanted below your pet's skin using a syringe. Once the microchip is implanted, your pet carries a unique identification number, which can be read by a microchip reader. Information related to your name address, and contact information is stored in a central database, accessible worldwide via the Internet. Information may be updated, if your address or other contact information is changed, without having to remove the chip or causing any discomfort to your pet.

Tattoos have been used for many years as a source of pet identification. An ID number is tattooed into an ear, and may be cross-referenced, at least locally, to find the pet owner. However, it should be noted that, like human tattoos, a pet tattoo may disperse under the skin and fade, making the ID number difficult or impossible to read. Also, local records may not be accessible if a pet becomes lost during a trip in another location.

ID tags on a collar may also be used to identify a pet, in an emergency. In many locations throughout the country, dogs and/or cats are required to be licensed by local authorities. In an emergency, ensure your pet is wearing a collar with up-to-date information tags, and that they are securely fastened to your pet's collar. If possible in an actual emergency, include an emergency contact number for the location where you will be if your pet becomes lost or is separated from you.

However, tags are not a comprehensive solution in an emergency, as tags or a collar may be torn off, or local records may not be accessible if a pet becomes lost during a trip away from home.

Consider creating an information sheet about your pet for reference purposes in an emergency, and store it in an easily accessible place in your home, or in your pet's emergency kit (see the previous section above).

Information, which may be useful, includes:

- **The location of your pet's emergency kit** (if stored separately from the information)

- **Habits and favourite hiding places** within your home

- **The name address and contact number of your pet's veterinarian**

- **The location and contact number for the nearest emergency veterinary clinic** in your area, if a medical emergency occurs after hours or on a holiday

- **Contact numbers for the local pet shelter**, pound and SPCA, if your pet becomes lost while you are absent

- **Current photos and a description of your pet**, if you become separated

- **A photocopy of your pet's medical records**, including any special medical conditions

- **Normal feeding schedules and food type**

- **A listing of any special behaviour problems**

Consider phoning motels and hotels in your area, and surrounding area, to determine whether any of them would allow pets to shelter with you on a temporary emergency basis if evacuation were required. Ask about any restrictions related to number, size or species of pet. Note the phone numbers and addresses for these motels or hotels in your emergency plan.

 ## Support network

Like humans who have special needs, pets may require a support network in an emergency situation.

The emergency may be as simple as you're not being able to make it home due to icy road conditions, and having a pet at home that requires feeding. In a major emergency where you have been required to evacuate your home, it may be a situation where your pet cannot be housed in the emergency shelter with you.

For localized, short term emergency conditions, consider finding relatives or trusted friends who live nearby, or a trusted neighbour who is comfortable and familiar with your pet(s) and provide them with a key to your home, to allow them access for feeding purposes in an emergency. Let them know something about your pet's particular habits, including favourite hiding places, to assist in finding the pet(s) quickly if required. Give them information about the location of your pet's emergency kit, in case they have need of it in an emergency.

If you live in a townhouse, condominium or apartment block that allows pets, consider providing the following information to the landlord, property manager or condominium board which may be useful to emergency agencies:

◉ **Your emergency contact information** and the name of an alternate emergency contact if an emergency involves your pet

◉ **Information about the pet**, including it's name, type or breed, and favourite places to hide in the home

◉ **Information about your pet(s) food requirements**, medications required or other special needs

◉ **Location of the pet's emergency kit** and other special equipment (eg. carrier)

◉ **Location of an emergency key** for entrance to the residence

◉ **A written letter giving signed permission for entry into the residence** to rescue your pet if required

Pre-planning for a major emergency where you and your pet must be evacuated from your home begins by finding an appropriate shelter location. Consider contacting friends or relatives who are outside of the immediate area, but close enough for easy access and ask them whether they would be willing to shelter your pet on a temporary basis, if an emergency did occur.

Items like allergies to pets and compatibility with existing pets in their home should be taken into account, when accessing the viability of this option in an emergency. If pets are already in the friend's or relatives home, consider bringing your pet over to the home to familiarize the pets with each other, and determine whether any behavioural problems would occur. The option of boarding your pet with a friend or relative may be less stressful than sheltering them in a kennel or temporary emergency animal shelter.

Your veterinarian, or a pet sitting organization, or the boarding kennel that you use regularly may also be able to provide potential shelter for your pets in an emergency or may be able to offer suggestions for other shelter locations in your local area. Keep your pets medical records up to date, and ensure your pet's shots are up to date. Some organizations will not accept a pet in an emergency unless you can provide proof of proper vaccinations.

It should be noted that in a major emergency, pet-sitting shelters, boarding kennels or veterinary clinics might be swamped with requests for service of this nature, making use of their services difficult or impossible. If this option is the only one available to you in an emergency, consider discussing it well in advance with the appropriate individuals providing these services.

For additional ideas, consider contacting your local animal shelter, humane society, or the emergency management agency in your community, to discuss outside options for boarding or housing animals in an emergency. If the emergency is widespread, and affects your whole community, government related options might not be available.

As with a support network for humans, try to have more than one individual involved in your pet's support network as one individual may be away at certain times, due to work related activities, holidays, or other activities which will not allow them to be immediately available in an emergency. Consider having two to three individuals if possible, to assist in your pet support network locally, and try to find two to three options for boarding your pet in an emergency, if at all possible.

 If you must evacuate and bring a pet ...

⊚ **Try to leave with your pet well in advance of any mandatory evacuation**. You may only have minutes to evacuate if an emergency is imminent. Rescue transport vehicles may only have limited space and the safety of humans is the priority. You may be required to leave your pet behind if no space is available

⊚ **Ensure that you bring your pet's emergency supplies with you**, including any special items which are not normally stored with their kit

⊚ **Ensure your pet has its identification collar on, as appropriate**

If you must leave your pet behind ...

Your pet trusts you to provide a safe and protective environment in normal situations. As mentioned previously the best and safest option in an emergency is to take your pet with you out of harm's way.

If you have absolutely no option but to leave your pet(s) behind in an emergency situation, consider some elements which will assist them in their survival, including:

⊚ **Bring pets into a sheltered location immediately** if severe weather is anticipated. Animals have instincts about changes preceding a storm, which may cause them to flee or isolate themselves, making them difficult to locate. Never leave a pet tied up outside if a storm is anticipated

⊚ **Never leave a pet chained outside** if you evacuate and leave them behind

⊚ **For household pets, try to find a safe location to leave them**, considering the following criteria:

- **Try to shelter them in an easy to clean area**, such as a utility room or bathroom

- **Avoid rooms with windows which could shatter**, or other hanging objects such as pictures or wall hangings which can fall or shatter spreading broken glass or other potentially dangerous debris

- **Avoid sheltering pets in basement rooms**, which could be flooded in an emergency. If pets must be sheltered in ground level rooms, put them in rooms with higher counters or other areas they can escape to

- **Separate dogs and cats and shelter them separately.** Even if your dogs and cats normally get along, the stress of an emergency situation may cause them to act in an unusual and potentially aggressive manner. Avoid keeping other small pets confined with your dog or cat
- **Leave familiar items in the room** such as favourite bedding and toys
- **Leave at least a two to three day supply of dry non-perishable food.** Avoid leaving soft food, thinking you will provide a treat for your pet. Soft food can turn rancid or spoil quickly, making the rest of the food smell or taste unpalatable. Try to leave the food in a container that your pet cannot overturn
- **Try to have access to a supply of fresh water.** Leave water in a sturdy container that cannot be overturned easily. If a faucet and basin or container is present in the room, consider opening the faucet slightly, to allow water to drip into the container. Some animals may be able to obtain water from a partially filled bathtub
- **Provide extra litter for your pet cats, as far from food as possible,** and appropriate sanitary arrangements for other pets
- **Consider leaving a note on a visible area** like the main door of your home, indicating that a pet has been left in the home, due to evacuation. Indicate the type of pet, the pet's name and the location where it has been left. Leave a contact number where you can be reached as well as an alternate emergency contact. Consider leaving the contact number for your veterinarian as well

After an emergency where a pet is involved ...

Most animals like dogs and cats are territorial by nature. After an emergency, pets may find conditions in their territory have altered. Familiar scents and landmarks may not be present. Strange sounds may be heard. Downed power lines or spilled chemicals may be present. Dangerous animals such as poisonous snakes may have traveled into a normally safe area. For a variety of reasons your pet may become confused, lost or frightened.

Maintain close contact with your pet after the emergency is over. For household pets, that are usually allowed outdoors, avoid allowing them outside, if possible, until you are sure of conditions in the surrounding area. If a pet must go outdoors, chain or leash them and confine them in a controlled fenced area if possible.

Animals may undergo behavioural changes after an emergency, due to anxiety or stress. Normally quiet and friendly animals may become belligerent or aggressive to family members, other persons or pets. Monitor their behaviour closely, and isolate them on a temporary basis, if required. If behaviours do not improve, seek advice and assistance from your veterinarian or other animal behaviour specialists.

PERSONAL PREPAREDNESS – PANDEMICS

The annual influenza season (commonly known as the "flu" season) is a regular occurrence every year (normally November to March), with the inevitable cold or flu-like symptoms, which can affect a single individual, or an entire family, resulting in lost time from work, school or other activities which are normally undertaken. The flu can last a few days or even more than a week, depending on the patient and their general health. While infected individuals normally recover quickly, there is always the potential for mortality in the elderly, the infirm, or in infants, due to limited ability to fight off disease.

If large numbers of individuals are affected quickly in one area, the resulting condition is known as an **EPIDEMIC**.

A **PANDEMIC**, while infrequent, is a much more serious condition. An average of three recorded pandemics, (one major, two minor), have occurred every century, for at least the last four centuries.

A pandemic may be defined as a widespread epidemic. The effects of the pandemic may be global in scale, affecting all portions of the world simultaneously. Unlike an epidemic, the effects of a pandemic may also be more rapid, lethal, and wide spread, with serious illness and high potential for mortality in all age groups, and all individuals affected, not just the elderly, young or infirm.

A pandemic can occur for the following reasons, including:

- **Rapid spread of a new virus** which has not been encountered before, through a population with no immunity

- **Rapid spread of a virus which has appeared before**, historically, for which a population has lost immunity

- **Rapid spread of a virus, indigenous to a local area**, through individuals traveling globally to other areas, carrying and spreading the virus

Unlike previous occurrences of pandemics, the onset of a modern pandemic may be exacerbated by the rapid pace of travel in the 21st century, allowing infected individuals to travel literally around the world in a day, potentially spreading the pandemic to all corners of the globe within hours or days, as opposed to weeks or months historically.

While a pandemic can have a serious impact on individuals and their families on a micro scale, its effects may be widespread and severe over an extended time period, affecting everyone, even if they are not actually infected with the disease. The effects would be most severely felt in urban areas, with high-density populations, as the world has never faced a major pandemic with populations this large or so geographically concentrated within urban centres.

With an unknown number of persons who may be infected at any time, in a wide variety of professions and services, and the prevalence of providing many services and supplies "just in time" to required areas, wide reaching effects could occur. Temporary breakdowns in food delivery, unavailability of personnel to repair electrical, heating and water services and potential disruption to public order is not outside the realm of possibility. Most severely affected may be health services, as the sheer number of individuals with extremely serious conditions, which require immediate treatment, could overwhelm hospitals.

With all these factors in mind, personal preparedness for a pandemic can represent a serious and real concern to all of us.

Pandemic Pre-Planning

Some considerations for planning for a pandemic include:

- **Making a will, or ensuring your will is up to date**, if something does occur

- **Ensuring your family has sufficient life insurance with well established companies** to cover contingencies if something occurs as a result of the pandemic

- **Getting a flu shot, to protect against the current seasonal flu.** This most likely will not protect you against a pandemic flu, but could limit the possibility of getting a seasonal flu, and therefore seriously weakening your condition if you also contract a pandemic flu

- **Getting a vaccination to protect against pneumonia** as viral pneumonia infections can be one of the largest causes of mortality in a pandemic

- **Considering staying with relatives or friends in a rural area** during a pandemic, to limit effects to you and your family. This may need to be planned well in advance, and implemented quickly if a pandemic is occurring, as many communities may try to limit influx of individuals from urban centres in a pandemic

- **Learn simple medical skills** such as taking a pulse, blood pressure, temperature and respiratory rate, if home care is required. Request assistance from your doctor or a nurse to develop these simple skills

- **Have information available** to assist you in home care, if needed

Supplies and equipment

In addition to the basic emergency supplies described previously (see Preparedness in the Home), you may wish to stock up on specific supplies, which may be useful for home care, well in advance of a pandemic.

These supplies include, but not are limited to:

- **Table salt** – 1 kilogram (2.2 pounds)
- **Table sugar** – 5 kilograms (11 pounds)
- **Baking soda** – 500 grams (1.1 pounds)
- **Household bleach** – 10 litres (2.5 U.S. gallons)
- **Tums** – 500 tablets

- **Acetaminophen** (Tylenol) – 500 mg (200 tablets)

- **Ibuprofen** (Advil) – 200 mg (200 tablets)

- **Caffeinated tea**, dry loose – 1 kilogram (2.2 pounds)

Useful equipment for home care of individuals in a pandemic can include, but not be limited to:

- **An electronic thermometer,** or any thermometer you are able to read

- **A battery operated blood pressure monitor** (make sure you understand how to use the monitor correctly)

- **A notebook to record vital signs**, fluid intake and fluid output and other information

If a pandemic is predicted, you may also wish to increase emergency stockpiles of food, and other basic supplies in your home, from the normal of three to five days to two weeks to a month, as potential disruptions of supplies of basic necessities may occur. As with any other major emergency condition, a pandemic may cause panic buying to occur, quickly emptying the shelves of all supermarkets and stores of useable supplies in both the local and regional areas. Consider topping up your emergency food supplies at the onset of the usual winter flu season (November to March).

Abundant supplies of food requiring limited preparation should be considered, if disruptions to electricity and other utilities are likely. Additional supplies of spare batteries, fuels for alternative heating and cooking sources should also be considered.

Fill empty containers, bathtubs, and other large, clean vessels with water, in the event that disruptions occur to water supplies.

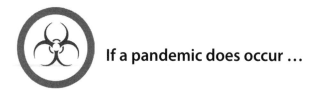

Conditions encountered in a pandemic will be similar to the normal flu season, in that individuals may contract the flu or not.

Some individuals may have natural immunity, or exhibit mild symptoms, while others may be severely or critically infected. Symptoms of exposure may not manifest themselves until two to five days after infection.

During a pandemic, items to consider can include but not be limited to:

⊚ **Monitoring yourself** and members of your family for signs of the flu:

- **Primary mild signs** – fever, sore throat, cough, runny nose, general aches and pains (similar to cold symptoms)
- **Secondary, severe signs** – headache, severe shivering, extreme weakness, nausea, vomiting, abdominal cramps, diarrhea (flu specific)
- **Critical, (potentially life threatening) signs** – respiratory tract infections, difficulty breathing, pneumonia (signs of secondary infection)

Even in a pandemic, the majority of cases will exhibit the mild or severe flu symptoms noted above.

⊚ **Monitoring news reports related to the pandemic**, and following any advice, instructions or directions given by health care authorities in the area

⊚ **Following any instructions given within your**

workplace, school or other areas, to limit transmission of the flu from person to person

If a member of your family comes down with the flu, items to consider can include but not be limited to:

- **Administering home care** to those who have come down with a severe but not critical infection

- **Seeking medical assistance immediately,** if a respiratory infection, pneumonia or other critical medical condition has developed in conjunction with the flu

---

NOTE:

In a pandemic, the sheer volume of flu cases will limit access to bed spaces, medical personnel and supplies, as health institutions will most likely be overwhelmed.

However, severe respiratory infections or pneumonia, especially coupled with a severe flu, are <u>critical conditions</u>, normally requiring access to advanced high technology medical resources and expert medical care to give a patient a chance of surviving the infection.

Caring for mildly or severely affected flu patients, where no other critical medical conditions are present, has been undertaken regularly within families for years, and can apply in a pandemic, in the same manner as any regular flu season. This care can be applied to everyone from very young children through to elderly patients. It is something everyone is capable of doing, with no medical skill required.

In all cases for home care of flu patients, the objectives are:

- **To keep the patient <u>well hydrated</u>** (eg. to maintain a sufficient volume of fluids within their body). Fever, sweating, and/or diarrhea can cause significant losses of water in the body

---

NOTE:

Making sure that the patient has plenty of fluids represents the <u>single most critical factor</u> in treating patients with the flu, as dehydration, due to rapid loss of fluids, can be fatal in a patient who could otherwise survive the infection, if no other critical medical conditions have also occurred.

Keeping patients hydrated can save a life!

Symptoms and signs of dehydration could include but not be limited to:

- **Weakness, headaches and fainting**
- **Dryness of the mouth** and decreased saliva
- **Lack of or very decreased urine output**
- **Dark and highly concentrated urine**
- **Sunken eyes** or loss of skin elasticity
- **Low blood pressure** sitting up or rising to a standing position
- **Fast pulse rate** when laying or sitting

If mild dehydration is developing, or severe dehydration has developed:

- **Administer fluids by mouth**, with patient assistance

- **Administer fluids drop by drop**, if needed, if patient is too ill to drink. Work up to using a teaspoon if possible, and continue until patient is able to have at least a litre (quart) of water (may take many hours for extremely sick patients)

- **Continue administering fluids regularly**, even if patient has been refreshed or revived

When administering fluids:

- **Serve hot or cold fluids** depending on the climate, patient's condition and whether they have a fever. Hot fluids may raise a patient's temperature even further. Patients with high fever might prefer a cool or even cold beverage

- **Water and juices** represent some of the best fluids for re-hydrating a patient. Ginger Ale or clear soft drinks (7-Up or Sprite) are also effective re-hydrating fluids, and provide some carbohydrates for energy. Gatorade or PowerAde or other sports beverages can also replenish some minerals lost from the blood and body through sweating and diarrhea. Jell-o or other gelatin solutions may also be used to provide additional fluids into the body

- **Try to provide 2-3 litres (quarts) of fluids every day** to patients experiencing dehydration, as a minimum, and provide more as required

NOTE:

An ORAL RE-HYDRATION SOLUTION (ORS) may be created from commonly available home supplies, or from supplies, which you have stockpiled for pandemic preparedness (See Supplies and Equipment above).

ORS contains similar ingredients to those provided in some intravenous solutions administered in a hospital, but may be taken orally, instead.

A typical formula is:
4 cups clean water (boiled or purified if required)*
3 tablespoons sugar or honey
½ tsp table salt

The ORS solution may be flavoured with other drinks or with lemon, mint or other herbs.

* Juice may be substituted instead of water, and sweeteners may be cut in half.

⊙ To keep a patient's <u>fever down and treat other symptoms of the flu</u> (body aches, chills, sore throat, headache)

NOTE:

A very high fever (> 40° C (104° F)) can cause seizures and brain damage and must be avoided. 37° C (98.6° F) represents normal body temperature.

- ◉ **If fever or other symptoms are developing**, or have developed:
  - **Use Ibuprofen or acetaminophen**, or both, in appropriate doses to help lower fever, reduce headache pain, and relieve sore throat symptoms, making the patient more comfortable
  - **Use towels, sponges, or other cloths and tepid or cool water**, to help lower body temperature
  - **Relieve sore throats with hot beverages** or gargling with salt water (be aware that hot beverages can increase body temperature and may exacerbate a fever
  - **Use hot caffeinated tea to relieve sore throats**, headaches and coughs. The stimulant effect of tea may also improve the patients sense of well-being

- ◉ To keep the patient <u>clean and dry</u>
  - **Try to change, wash and dry soiled garments and bedclothes on a regular basis** (may be difficult if electrical and water services are interrupted frequently). Wash in hot water using soap and chlorine bleach if possible
  - **Try to keep sickrooms and bathrooms clean** and in good condition. Wipe down hard surfaces using soap and water, then wipe down a second time with 1:10 bleach to water solution

- ◉ To keep the patient <u>warm and comfortable</u>
  - **A comfortable resting place** to lie down and continual reassurance of the patient will facilitate this process

⊚ **To keep the patient _fed_, when they become hungry again** (Flu will take appetite away, making the person not feel hungry)

Developing an appetite again is a marked sign of improvement in the individual. If they develop an appetite, provide foods that are appropriate based on their weakened condition. Solid foods will be difficult to digest for these patients at first, so provide a **clear liquid diet**, which gradually advances them through the following steps:

> **Step 1:** Provide Oral Re-hydration Solution (ORS), water, fruit juice, Jell-o, Gatorade or PowerAde, Ginger Ale, Sprite or tea (NOTE: this part of the diet is typically provided throughout the illness, to treat or prevent dehydration)

> **Step 2:** Add dry toast (no butter, margarine), items like white rice, cream of wheat, soda crackers or potatoes (without skin)

> **Step 3:** To steps above, add items like canned fruit and chicken noodle soup

> **Step 4:** To steps above, add poached eggs, baked chicken without skin, canned fish or meat

> **Step 5:** To steps above, add milk and other dairy products, margarine and butter, raw fruits and vegetables, and high fibre whole grain products

NEW AGE EMERGENCY PREPAREDNESS

With the advent of new technologies, many new items are available to consumers and may be used to enhance personal emergency preparedness.

Flashlights / spotlights

NightStar II Shake Flashlight
Garrity Hand Crank Flashlight

One of the most frequent problems, which people encounter in an emergency involving power loss, is dead or weak batteries in a flashlight, and no replacement batteries being available.

Flashlights are available on the market today that do not use any batteries as a source of power.

One type of alternate power source for flashlights operates on the principle of magnetic induction to generate electricity. Shaking the flashlight for 30-90 seconds generates power. This charges a capacitor built into the unit.

Low voltage light emitting diodes (LEDs) are used instead of light bulbs to provide a source of steady light for between five to fifteen minutes at a time, depending on the model. Additional charging of the flashlight is undertaken by shaking the flashlight again.

Dynamo based flashlights are also available, which use a mechanical dynamo that is operated by squeezing a handle or turning a crank for thirty to ninety seconds. The dynamo is used to charge a capacitor or battery in a manner similar to the magnetic induction flashlight described previously.

Performance for these types of flashlights is similar to those described previously.

Solar powered flashlights are also available, which use a small solar panel during daylight hours to charge a rechargeable battery. These flashlights are not very useful in a power blackout at night, if the flashlight has been kept in a dark area and batteries are in a discharged state. However, flashlights of this nature may be useful while camping, or in an extended power blackout, which lasts several days, if they are exposed to sunlight during daylight hours.

In addition, rechargeable spotlights are also available on the market, which can use both standard and LED light sources interchangeably, to provide either a constant source of bright light for a moderate period of time, or a steady source of less intense light for an extended period of time. Spotlights

Noma Dual Light Source Spotlight
LED / Xenon Bulbs

of this nature can flip between regular and LED light sources on a continuous basis, until the power source is depleted.

Light sticks

Lighting tubes, which operate on chemo luminescent principles (eg. mixing of chemicals to produce light), have been available on the market for many years for a variety of uses, including camping. These types of light sticks can also be used in an emergency as a source of temporary lighting.

Light sticks are normally constructed of plastic, and are operated by bending the stick to break a vial or seal in the stick, which is then shaken to mix the chemicals. The colour and brightness of the light produced is dependent on the types of chemicals used to produce the lighting effect. The amount of time that the light stick will continue to produce light can also vary from a few minutes to a few hours in length.

Light sticks have the advantage of producing a steady, if low quality light which is safe, and cannot overheat or provide an open ignition source that can start a fire. However, lighting of this nature also has disadvantages, as it cannot be varied in intensity, unless a shade is used around it. Also, once the chemical reaction has completed, the light stick cannot be used again, and must be disposed of properly.

 ## Radios

Like flashlights, portable radios are also available on the market, which can operate on renewable or rechargeable power sources, without any external power source or disposable batteries required.

Some of these radios are charged using a hand cranked dynamo system, while others are solar powered. In some cases, both of these alternate charging methods are available in the same package, providing options for both daylight and nighttime operation. In some models, disposable batteries, AC chargers and standard electrical power may also be used, if available.

NOTE:

Units using rechargeable nickel cadmium (NiCad) batteries can develop a "memory" if batteries remain on constant charge.

Blankets

As a byproduct of the space age, thermal blankets made of Mylar have been available for decades. These can be used in an emergency to provide shelter and warmth.

Standalone alternative power sources

iSun Corporation
5W Portable Solar Panel (closed)

Technology has now made readily accessible alternative power sources available to the consumer.

Solar panel solutions are now available from a variety of sources, which can provide steady sources of power, to recharge batteries, or run small electronic devices directly, while sunlight is available. These solar panels are available as fixed installations, which can be installed on a building, as well as portable panels, that can be carried to remote locations or stored in a vehicle for use as required.

In an emergency, small solar panels are available which generate sufficient power to charge or run a cellular phone, a GPS unit, or to run a battery charger for charging batteries for use in a flashlight, and an emergency radio.

iSun Corporation
5W Portable Solar Panel (open)

Power inverters

Motomaster Eliminator Digital Power Inverter 800 W

Power inverters are devices, which can convert direct current (DC) power generated by items such as a 12 volt vehicle battery to alternating current (AC), which is used as a power source for most electronic devices in a home.

These devices are now commonly available from retail electronic outlets, and camping supply companies, for use in operating televisions, radios, small power tools, VCRs, or portable computers and other common electronic devices, while in a remote area without line power.

In an emergency where normal electrical supplies are disrupted, power inverters of sufficient size may be used to recharge critical use battery systems, as well as running required electrical devices on a sporadic or on-going basis.

On-going use of a power inverter with a vehicle battery will require the vehicle to be run, to ensure that the vehicle battery is not completely drained. If charging a battery from a running vehicle in a garage, ensure that proper ventilation is present by opening the garage door, to prevent build-up of carbon monoxide or other toxic gases.

If the power emergency is expected to last for an extended period of time, consideration should be given to running electronics from your vehicle only as needed, to conserve vehicle fuel supplies for necessary uses.

Portable Power Packs

Standalone power packs are now readily available on the market, which may be used to power electrical devices, or to charge other power sources in an emergency.

Most of these devices have a built-in lead acid battery, which may be used on a long term basis, and may be charged numerous times without developing a memory, These devices can use a wide variety of charging sources, including plug-in to standard AC household current (using a

Xantrex Xpower
Powerpack Solar 300 W

charging adapter), plugging into a DC power source (such as a vehicle cigarette lighter / utility plug-in), or even a solar panel. In some cases, power packs are available that have the capability to charge from any of these sources interchangeably.

Power packs also have the capability to power a wide variety of devices, depending on the rating of the unit involved. Some power packs can only provide DC based power internally, while others have built-in power inverters, which can provide AC power to devices.

The amount of time that a device can be run on a power pack is highly dependent on the size of the battery in the unit, as well as the power requirements of the device plugged into the unit. Most power packs can power smaller devices (cell phones, GPS systems, radios, and sound devices), for an extended period of time.

Personal communicators

Low cost multi channel family radio service (FRS) personal communicators are now commonly available from most retail electronics outlets.

Motorola TalkAbout T7100 Personal Communicator

These small battery powered radio handsets operate on radio frequencies assigned for public use. With a point-to-point transmitting range of two to three kilometres these units are ideal for personal communications between two or more individuals over short ranges.

Unlike cellular phones, and other private radio services, personal communicators have no requirement for supplementary radio repeater towers, or radio licensing, making them attractive to consumers. Also personal communicators may be used outside areas where cellular service is available.

FRS radios have the same limitations as most point-to-point communication systems. Communications may be difficult in mountainous areas, or other areas where line of sight may be difficult to establish. These considerations should be taken into account, if you are looking at purchasing a FRS communication system.

Like other rechargeable electronic equipment, which use nickel cadmium (NiCad) batteries, these radio sets should be discharged completely, prior to recharging. This will prevent the batteries from developing a "memory", which will shorten the time that the communicator can be used without recharge.

Some FRS units use nickel metal hydride (NiMH) batteries, which have fewer problems with developing memory from continuous recharging.

In an emergency, FRS radios may be used as an alternative to stay in touch with family members in the immediate area, even if telephone service is unavailable.

NOTE:

It should be remembered that public radio frequencies in a major urban centre would most likely be jammed with people attempting to communicate in some manner on a priority basis in a major emergency.

If telephone communications are knocked out or jammed with calls, FRS systems may be used to attempt to communicate with emergency support agencies and get help.

For this reason, limit your communications as much as possible, and use your communicator(s) only as absolutely necessary.

YOUR SILENCE MAY SAVE A LIFE!

Consider assisting persons trying to communicate a request for medical aid, or other assistance, and relay information to appropriate authorities, if they are personally out of range.

Battery back-ups

American Power Corporation (APC)
Back-UPS 725 Battery Back-up

Uninterruptible power supplies (UPS) were originally developed to protect critical computer and other electrical based infrastructure in industry, large municipalities, and government agencies, where systems knocked out by a power outage could severely affect the safety of personnel, the public, or cause damage to property or the environment.

With the widespread use of computers in the home, small UPS systems for personal use are readily available in most retail stores selling office supplies to the public.

UPS units contain a battery, which is kept continuously charged when the UPS is connected to the normal home power supply. When a power outage occurs, the battery provides sufficient power to allow the unit to continue to operate in a normal manner on a short-term basis, to read and to enable the unit to be shut down properly, preventing damage to sensitive components or loss of data.

Many battery back-ups also contain surge protection circuitry, which limits damage to electrical equipment caused by power surges or brownouts. UPS units may be used in conjunction with a separate surge protection system, to provide additional protection in an emergency.

Battery back-up systems may also be used on other sensitive electrical systems (eg. televisions, audio/visual equipment, to protect this equipment from damage, and allow components to be shutdown appropriately in an emergency power outage.

It should be noted that most personal battery back-up systems will provide only five to ten minutes of additional power in a power outage, depending on the make of UPS, and the capacity of the battery. However, if your power needs require extended use of equipment if an emergency occurs, heavy duty battery back-ups are now readily available, with sufficient power to run larger devices for extended periods of time.

If you choose to get a battery back-up unit to protect valuable electronics in your home, the unit should have sufficient capacity to continue to run the computer or electronic device when on battery. If insufficient power capacity is present in the UPS, the connected device will immediately shut down in a power outage. If you are unclear as to how large a battery back-up capacity is required for the device you wish to protect, consult with sales representatives or review manufacturer's information prior to making your purchase.

NOTE:

The intention of most personal UPSs is <u>not</u> to allow you to continue to play a video game, or continue to watch a movie until the end during a power blackout – it is to give you sufficient time to shut down the electronic device without damage.

The same type of damage to your electronic device may still result, if your battery back up becomes completely discharged, and stops running with the electrical device still on.

Like all batteries, batteries in a UPS device will eventually become too old to maintain a charge, and require replacement. Many of these devices have now been designed to allow easy replacement of the battery. Batteries in a UPS should be checked regularly, as part of your normal emergency preparedness checks in the home.

Many battery back-up systems purchased to protect a computer system have the ability to shutdown the computer automatically if no one is present. Appropriate software and special cables may be required to allow the battery back up to communicate with the computer system. Consult with a sales representative where you purchased the UPS unit, or contact the manufacturer of the UPS, to determine whether this option exists.

Water purification devices

Water purification filters have been available for some time for use on faucets, to enhance purity of urban or rural water supplies. These devices can remove many contaminants in water, based on their specific design. Similar portable filtration systems are also available for use in camping.

Filters of this nature may be used in an emergency, in addition to methods recommended by local emergency officials, to enhance the purity of potentially contaminated water.

It should be noted that any filtration device has a limited life, based on the type of medium in the filter, and the filtration principle used. Filters should not be used past their recommended lifetime, as contamination can pass through the filter. If heavy contamination is present in a water supply, filters may quickly loose their effectiveness and may need to be changed frequently.

USEFUL REFERENCES

Many useful sources of reference information are available in print, on the Internet and through local emergency preparedness agencies in your community, which were used as reference sources in preparing this handbook. Some of these sources may be of some use to you in your own personal emergency preparedness activities.

Many of these sources are available in electronic form, and are accessible normally through the Internet. However, it should be noted that in an emergency, electronic sources may not be readily available if power supplies are affected. You may wish to consider printing out important information which you want available for reference, and put this information in your emergency kit for future consideration.

As information on this subject is constantly changing, we have not included links to various documents within this book. However, a compendium of reference information of this nature is available on-line at our website at:

www.paladinenvironmental.com

I am always interested in any new tips on personal emergency preparedness that others may have. If you wish to submit comments, tips, and or questions, please contact me through the contacts on the website above.

May all your personal emergency preparedness efforts be successful, and help you keep you, your family and others safe in an emergency.

Mark Szkolnicki